G000245414

A TRAGEDY
OF ERRORS

The story of

Grace Murray

the woman whom John Wesley loved and lost

G . M . B E S T

NEW ROOM PUBLICATIONS
BRISTOL

NEW ROOM PUBLICATIONS

A Tragedy of Errors
First published 2016

New Room Publications is an imprint of Tangent Books
Unit 5.16 Paintworks
Bristol BS4 3EH
0117 972 0645
www.tangentbooks.co.uk
Email: richard@tangentbooks.co.uk

ISBN 978-1-910089-37-8

Author: Gary Best

Design: Joe Burt (www.wildsparkdesign.com)

Also by G. M. Best

Non-Fiction
Seventeenth-Century Europe Documents and Debates
Continuity and Change: A History of Kingswood School 1748-1998
Charles Wesley: A Biography
Shared Aims
Transformed Lives

Historical Guides
John Wesley: a tercentenary commemorative study
The Seven Sisters
Susanna Wesley
Charles Wesley

Musical
Marley's Ghosts

Novels
Oliver Twist Investigates
Wuthering Heights Revisited
The Jacobite Murders
The Barchester Murders

Contents

Susanna Wesley, mother of John Wesley (from print in the New Room)

John Wesley And Marriage

Some historians have argued that much of the emotional angst that John Wesley faced in his dealings with women stemmed from his relationship with his mother, Susanna. As an example of that they have quoted the remark that he made when he was six or seven year old that he would never marry because it was impossible to find a woman to equal her. In itself this is the kind of comment a number of young children make, but, in Wesley's case, as a young man he certainly did compare other women with his mother and usually found them wanting. In his opinion they lacked Susanna's spiritual understanding and self-effacing dedication to living a perfect Christian life and they were unwilling to take second place to what he felt God wanted him to do. This was a particularly important consideration for John because his mother had instilled in him that he had been saved from the fire that engulfed their home in 1709 so he could one day fulfil a special divine purpose.

There is no evidence to suggest Susanna thought John should never marry, but she certainly would have told him that he should not acquire any wife who might stop him devoting all his energies to serving God. In this context it has been argued that Susanna set a personal example by deliberately keeping John at 'a measured emotional distance' and that this encouraged him to suppress his emotions.[1] When he was at university, for example, she told him that she was glad he was unable to come home because it was better for her 'to have as few attachments to the world as possible' and she corrected him for signing one of his letters to her 'your affectionate dutiful son' with the following words:

'The conclusion of your letter is very kind. That you were ever dutiful, I very well know. But I know myself enough to rest satisfied with a moderate degree of your affection. It would be unjust in me to desire the love of anyone.'[2]

It would be wrong, however, to attribute John's thinking on marriage solely to Susanna. Although the influence of his father, Samuel, has been less commented upon, there is no doubt that he strongly advised that both John and Charles should never marry. He told them it had wrecked his own career because the financial demands involved in sustaining his wife and children had forced him to remain as rector of Epworth, a role far beneath his talents.

The views of his parents did not prevent John enjoying the company of women and flirting with them when he was at university, but he found it difficult to handle the sexual feelings that this aroused:

'Oft as thro' giddy youth I rov'd,
And danced along the flowery way,
By chance or thoughtless passion mov'd,
An easy, unsuspicious prey
I fell, while Love's envenomed dart

1 See J.P. Briggs & J.Briggs, Unholy Desires, Inordinate Affections, Connecticut Review Spring 1991. This article argues that Wesley's relationships with women were affected by his 'thwarted longing for emotional acceptance and intimacy with his mother'.

2 14 May 1727 JW Letter book 1724-9 John Rylands Library

Thrilled thro' my veins, and tore my heart.'[3]

He studied why the Church had for so many centuries expected its clergy to take a vow of celibacy and he drew the conclusion it was because of the 'taint upon the mind necessarily attending the marriage-bed'.[4] In other words, it encouraged immoral thoughts. After his ordination as a presbyter at the age of twenty-five, he assumed he should take a vow of celibacy. Increasingly from then on he argued that marriage would only serve to distract him from giving a 100% commitment to God and that it was preferable for him to spend what little money he had on feeding the hungry and clothing the naked than on sustaining a wife and children. He later wrote of his determination to put God first:

> 'At length, by sad experience taught,
> Firm I shook off the abject yoke;
> Abhor'd his sweetly-poisonous draught,
> Thro' all his wily fetters broke;
> Fixt my desires on things above,
> And languisht for Celestial Love.'[5]

John's abilities and status inevitably attracted unmarried women and, because he liked their company, there was almost continuous gossip about him and his links with this or that female. Much has been written in particular about his early love affair with the eighteen-year old Sophy Hopkey, whom he met and courted when he was a missionary in the colony of Georgia. John records how he groaned under 'the weight of unholy desires' and was reduced to drawing lots

---

3 JW's poem on Grace Murray. For full text see the Epilogue.

4 JWLL pg 67. It was easy to argue this. St Paul, for example, stated in I Cor 7 that an unmarried person thought first of pleasing God but a married person thought first of pleasing his wife.

5 JW's poem on Grace Murray.

to see if he should marry her or not. However, months passed and no proposal was forthcoming. In the end her uncle decided John was simply playing with her affections and he forced Sophy to marry someone else. Only then did John realise how much he loved her:

'I walked up and down, seeking rest, but finding none… God let loose my inordinate affection upon me, and the poison thereof drank up my spirit. I was… in the sharpest pain I ever felt. 'To see her no more!' That thought was the piercing of a sword. It was not to be borne – nor shaken off. I was weary of the world, of light, of life… [God] forsook me. I could not pray. Then indeed the snares of death were about me: the pains of hell overtook me.' [6]

This led him to go public on his feelings. He refused to let Sophy take communion because he said she had sinned in not marrying him. The colonists alleged that he upset her so much that she miscarried with her first child. In the wake of this disaster Sophy's uncle had Wesley put on trial on a variety of charges and this forced John to flee America. As a consequence he vowed never again to put a woman first:

'Is there a thing beneath the sun
that strives with Thee my heart to share?
Ah, tear it thence, that Thou alone
May'st reign unrivall'd Monarch there:
From earthly loves I must be free
Ere I can find repose in Thee.'[7]

---

6 W.R. Ward & R. Heizenrater (edit), Journal & Diaries 1735-38 , Vol 8 Works, Clarendon Press 1988
7 John's translation whilst he was in Savannah of a German hymn by Gerhard Tersteegen

And John told the early Methodist lay preachers in no uncertain terms that he wanted them to remain single if they were not already married.

It was not until he was forty that John began seriously questioning whether his promotion of a celibate life was correct. It is easy to see what led him to think he might be wrong. There were enough married preachers for him to see that, if a person married the right wife, then she could become a support and not a hindrance to serving God. It was also the case that most of the clergy who supported him were married. It was as his resolve to remain single weakened that he decided God had been preparing Grace Murray, the housekeeper at the Orphan House in Newcastle, to become the perfect wife for him, one who would strengthen and not weaken his ministry:

> 'Born on the wings of sacred hope
> Long had I soar'd, and spurn'd the ground;
> When panting for the mountain-top
> My soul a kindred spirit found;
> By heaven intrusted to my care,
> The daughter of my faith and prayer.
>
> In early dawn of life, serene,
> Mild, sweet and tender was her mood:
> Her pleasing form spoke all within
> Soft and compassionately good:
> List'ning to every wretch's care,
> Mixing with each her friendly tear.'[8]

The story of John's resulting affair with Grace Murray and how

---

8 JW's poem on Grace Murray.

Charles Wesley prevented their marriage by persuading Grace to marry John Bennet, who was one of the key Methodist lay preachers, has long fascinated historians, but most have tended to view John as the victim and been hugely critical of the behaviour and actions of the others involved. Grace has been described as 'impetuous, imperious, and probably a little unstable'[9] and as an 'uneducated, vain, fickle, selfish and presuming' flirt[10], even though this does not tie in with either John Wesley's or John Bennet's view of her. Bennet has been dismissed as 'a cheat'[11] and 'a treacherous, unfriendly man'[12], even though Charles Wesley, George Whitefield and other contemporaries consistently praised his character. Charles has been accused of over-reacting to gossip and acting out of personal reasons. It has been alleged, for example, that he wanted John to remain single so he could retain the income his own wife required, and that both he and his wife were too snobbish to want to have Grace as their sister-in-law.[13] All these accusations have tended to obscure rather than clarify what really happened because they either ignore or do not pay enough attention to the fact that John Wesley was just as much to blame for what happened.

Today, after decades of relative historical neglect, Grace Murray is beginning to receive more recognition as 'a strong-willed, capable and dedicated woman worthy of a distinguished place in the annals of early Methodism'.[14] What emerges from this study is a remarkable woman – a pioneer female class leader and preacher, who, throughout her life, had to come to terms not only with the doubts and fears that can beset Christians at times, but also with the prejudices of her

9 R.E.Davies, Methodism, Epworth, 1960 pg 54

10 L. Tyerman, Life and Times of JW, Hodder & Stoughton 1890 Vol II pg 55-6

11 ibid

12 C.E. Vullimany, John Wesley, Bles 1933 pg 214

13 See G. Lloyd, Charles Wesley and the Struggle for Methodist Identity, OUP 2008.

14 S.R. Valentine, John Bennet and the Origins of Methodism, Scarecrow Press 1997 pg 235

day. Dr Johnson represented those well when he quipped: 'A woman preaching is like a dog walking on its hind legs. It is not done well; but you are surprised to find it done at all.'[15] What comes across most strongly in Grace's writings is her acute awareness of her own failings and her abiding faith in the redemptive love of God. When she knew she was approaching death she wrote to her son:

> 'God did wonders for me all my life. I have been astonished and overwhelmed with a sense of his love to me the chief of sinners, the most unfaithful and unprofitable of all his servants.'[16]

Her character makes it all the more understandable why John Wesley was hit so hard by her loss and why he struggled to understand why God had not permitted him to marry her:

> 'Unsearchable thy judgments are,
> O Lord, a bottomless abyss!
> Yet sure thy love, thy guardian care,
> O'er all thy works extended is.
> O why didst thou the blessing send?
> Or why thus snatch away my friend?'[17]

The main outcome of Grace's marriage to John Bennet has usually been portrayed as being John Wesley's disastrous marriage on the rebound to Molly Vazeille, but of far more significance was the divide her loss created between John and Charles. That had huge and important repercussions on the way in which Methodism was subsequently to develop.

After the initial trauma was over both John Wesley and Grace

15 James Boswell, The Life of Samuel Johnson, New York 1844 pg 205

16 ibid

17 JW's Poem on Grace Murray.

Murray came to believe that it was God who had prevented their marriage. In a more secular age, it seems preferable to explain what happened by looking at the actions of people involved and using the evidence available. This book tries to do exactly that and what emerges is a tragedy of errors for which all the protagonists can be held equally responsible. John Wesley, Grace Murray, John Bennet, and Charles Wesley all did what they did for the best, if at times misguided, motives. Whether the hand of God can also be seen in what happened I leave to the reader's judgement.

Gary Martin Best
March 2016

John Wesley painted by Nathaniel Hone and engraved by Bland (from print in the New Room)

George Whitefield preaching in 1742 painted by John Wollaston (by permission of National Portrait Gallery)

1

GRACE'S EARLY LIFE

Grace was born in Newcastle-upon-Tyne on 18 January 1716. We know nothing of her parents, Robert and Grace Norman, except that they were not wealthy and Grace says they were 'much distracted with worldly cares and business'.[18] Newcastle at that time was still very much as it had been built in medieval times. Most of its 20,000 inhabitants lived within the old city walls and the one stone bridge that provided access across the river was lined with shops and houses that dated back to the fourteenth century. Newcastle's main function was as a seaport, trading on coal and the products of a variety of local industries (such as lead, glass, pottery, bricks, and cutlery). Most of the people living there were very poor and uneducated. Given the fact her parents paid for Grace to go to school, her family were better off than most and therefore not as low in status as some historians have suggested.

The Norman family were members of the parish church of St Andrew's, which was the oldest of the four churches in the city. It traced its origins back to Anglo-Saxon times. Grace was christened in the church on 23 January. From its records, it would appear that she had four brothers and four sisters who were also christened there. They were named Ann (Dec 1703), Dorothy (Nov 1705), Stephen (January 1708), John (February 1711), Robert (September 1713), Eleanor (September 1718), Cuthbert (June 1721) and Margaret (May

1725).[19] The curate there since 1705 had been Thomas Shadforth.[20] Either he or more probably Robert Norman must have laid a great emphasis on the hellfire that awaited sinners. Grace records she was so much brought up to fear God's wrath that at the age of four she suffered terrifying visions of Him coming down to judge the world:

'I was much terrified till I thought he smiled upon me, on which my fears vanished away. From that time thoughts of death and judgement were often strong upon my mind, which made me earnest to serve God and careful to avoid whatever I believed displeasing to him.'[21]

From the age of six she was made to regularly study the Bible and she says she liked going to Church and was more religious than her brothers and sisters. One day when she was seven she felt God's presence so strongly when she was inside St Andrew's that the experience stuck with her for the rest of her life:

'I felt my soul overpowered with the love of God. And I loved all mankind. All my affections seemed changed. I wanted to be there always. These impressions remained upon my mind for a long time and indeed were never wholly effaced.'[22]

After this she gave away whatever money she had to the poor, and anything else that she could spare. Sometimes she even stole some of the food intended for the family in order to feed neighbours who otherwise would starve. What she says she lacked was an

19 The records use 'Elnor' as spelling for Eleanor and 'Margrett' for Margaret.

20 Ordained in 1690, Shadforth had been a preacher thoroughout the diocese of Durham and a curate at Sedgefield and Brancepeth before being appointed at St Andrew's.

21 JWLL pg 15-16. She says her father 'spoke to me early of the things of God'.

22 JWLL pg 16

understanding of the true nature of Christ – she saw him just as being a very good man who had 'suffered wrongly'. [23]

Thomas Shadforth died in 1724 and was replaced by John Ellison, whose father was vicar of St Nicholas' Church in Newcastle.[24] At much the same time Grace's childlike faith was weakened because the school to which she was sent taught dancing (alongside music and needlework). As a consequence her desire for 'heavenly things' was replaced by a love of dress and company and what others chose to see as 'innocent diversions'.[25] Dancing became what she later called her 'darling sin'.[26] She also discovered that she possessed a fine singing voice, which people found enchanting. As a consequence by the time she was a teenager she had largely ceased attending church. However, what she had acquired, in the words of one historian, was 'superior personal accomplishments, united to a mind cultivated by education, and an imagination brilliant and lively in the highest degree.'[27]

At the age of sixteen she started going out with a young man and she says that this made her grow ever more 'cooler to the things of God'.[28] Getting married was top of most women's agenda but Grace had no wish to lose her freedom. To her parents' frustration, she declined marriage when her suitor proposed to her two years later. Instead she left home in the summer of 1734 to go and live with one of her older sisters, who had moved to London. There she says she was treated like a child and was instantly 'swallowed up in worldly pleasures and diversions'.[29] She took up employment

23 ibid

24 He remained there till his death in 1766 and then his son took over.

25 JWLL pg 17

26 GBM pg 2

27 A.C.H. Seymour, Life and Times of Selina Hastings, Countess of Huntingdon, Simpkin & Marshall 1844 Vol I pg 45

28 JWLL pg 17

29 JWLL pg 18. Grace does not name which of her sisters it was.

as a serving maid in the house of an East India merchant and not long afterwards fell in love. On 13 May 1736, at the age of twenty, she married a mariner called Alexander Murray in a relatively new church in Stepney known as Saint George in the East.[30]

Stepney at that time was still semi-rural, but it was not far from the riverside docks of Shadwell and Ratcliff, from which most London registered ships sailed. This area, which was like a vast transit camp, was known as 'Sailortown'. Its many lodging houses were over-crammed with sailors on leave and there were countless bars and brothels. Understandably the area had a reputation for lawlessness and vice. Also nearby was Wapping, which was a centre not only for fitting and victualling the ships but also for boatbuilding and mast-making and for producing ships' instruments. It was also the location of 'Execution Dock', a place for public hangings. Its gibbet was so constructed that the bodies of those hung on it were submerged by incoming tides until it was judged time to cut them down.

Grace says that her husband was a sea captain and that he came from a Scottish family that had suffered much as a consequence of supporting the Jacobite cause.[31] The clan Murray traced its ancestry back to the twelfth century and it took its name from the one-time Scottish kingdom of Moray. It had (and still has) many branches. The clan had fought in both the 1715 and 1719 rebellions under the command of William Murray, Marquess of Tullibardine, who was the son of the Duke of Atholl. He was later to return to Scotland to help initiate the 1745 rebellion in favour of Bonnie Prince Charlie, and his younger brother, Lord George Murray, became the commander

---

30 It was one of six churches designed by Nicholas Hawksmoor and built between 1714 and 1729 in response to an Act of Parliament in 1711, which authorised the creation of fifty new churches in London.

31 This was the name given to those who supported the rights of 'the old Pretender' – the son of James II (who had been deposed in 1688 because of his Catholicism) and the father of Bonnie Prince Charlie.

of the Prince's army and the man behind its early victories.[32] After the failure of the 1719 rebellion, Alexander's father and uncles had been judged traitors. Their estates had been confiscated and they had been banished. The impoverished Alexander was forced to earn his living as a seaman.

Murray had to go back to sea just three or four days after the wedding. When Grace realised she was pregnant, she returned to her parents' home in Newcastle, but she says 'my husband was always before my eyes and engrossed all my thoughts'.[33] Fretting over whether he would return safely home led her to miscarry. She travelled back to London as soon as she heard his ship had returned. As an old woman Grace looked back on that journey as an occasion when God intervened to save her life. A neighbour, who also needed to travel to London, suggested they go together and book their passage on a particular ship, one of a convoy of about forty vessels. Grace insisted they should board a different one after she had a strong premonition that the ship her neighbour had chosen was doomed. Her fear proved correct:

'We had just got over the bar into the sea when a storm arose and scattered us widely from each other. The storm began about seven o'clock in the morning, and we were in it till nine at night. Two men were continually at the pumps, and two at the helm. It pleased God we got into the Humber, where we lay five days before we sailed again... When we arrived [in London], we found that eight ships had been lost, among which was that in which my friend had agreed to go, and every soul therein perished! Praise the Lord, O my soul, and forget not all his benefits! This

---

32 After the Prince's defeat at the Battle of Culloden, William Murray was imprisoned in the Tower of London, where he died, and George fled to the continent, dying in Holland in 1760. Some of clan Murray fled to America to escape the persecution and there is still a very active Murray Clan Society of North America.

33 JWLL pg 18

was the Lord's doing, and it is still marvellous in mine eyes.' [34]

She says she and Alexander then had four happy months together during which she came to worship him more than she worshipped God. She became pregnant again and on this occasion he made sure he was at home to support her in the later stages of her pregnancy, rather than letting her risk another miscarriage. According to the parish records of Saint George in the East, the couple's first child was baptised Susanna on 19 March 1738.[35] After this Murray went to sea again, leaving Grace and the baby in the care of her sister and brother-in-law. When the child was about fourteen months old Grace received news that her husband was ill in Portsmouth. She went to nurse him, taking the infant Susanna with her. They stayed in lodgings for six weeks. Grace says their landlady was very religious and she held prayers with her two daughters in her chamber twice each day for Alexander's recovery. This was not unusual behaviour. The Church encouraged women to pray regularly and to teach their children, and, if they were wealthy, their servants, to join in with the prayers. Observing the family's devotions made Grace realise just how much she had moved away from having a spiritual life of her own:

'This put me upon serious reflections on my past and present life and, upon earnest prayer that God would enable me to serve him, and supply me in whatever was wanting.' [36]

As soon as Alexander Murray was fit enough to travel, they returned

---

34 This is a recollection from her diary 19 Sept 1796 GBM pg 65

35 The parish church records give the date as 19 March 1737 but that is because it used the Julian Calandar in which the new year commenced on 25 March. It was not till 1751 that Parliament formally agreed Britain should use the Gregorian Calendar, which uses 1 January.

36 JWLL pg 19

to their home in Stepney in May 1739. This coincided with the time when the recently ordained George Whitefield had just commenced preaching virtually every evening on Kennington Common. Born in Gloucester, Whitefield had gone to Pembroke College, Oxford, and there become a member of a religious society run by John and Charles Wesley. John was a tutor at Lincoln College and Charles a student at Christ Church College. Other students had mocked them, calling them various names, including 'the Holy Club' and 'Methodists' because of their methodical approach to Christian living. Since then both Whitefield and the Wesleys had undertaken missionary work in America, and, at the outset of 1739 they and four other former Oxford Methodists had vowed to create a religious revival. In Whitefield's case this had led him to commence open-air preaching first in Bristol and then in London and he had persuaded John Wesley to join him in that activity, even though the church authorities opposed it.

Kennington Common was the haunt of prostitutes, thieves, and beggars, and a place where brutal brawls and mob violence were commonplace. Whitefield had first preached there on 29 April to a crowd that he estimated contained thirty thousand people:

'Let not the adversaries say I have thrust myself out. No, they have thrust me out. And since the self-righteous men of this generation count themselves unworthy, I go out into the highways and hedges, and compel harlots, publicans, and sinners to come in, that my Master's house may be filled. They who are sincere will follow after me to hear the Word of God.'[37]

Such was his success that every day he says he drew never less than a crowd of ten thousand and on one occasion it was as high as fifty

37 GW Journal 25 April 1739. Banner of Truth Trust edition 1965 pg 259.

thousand:

> 'The people were melted down very much at the preaching of the Word and put up heavy prayers for my temporal and eternal welfare... I offered Jesus Christ to all who could apply Him to their hearts by faith.'[38]

Many of the clergy at this time were making out that Whitefield was a madman. Grace says in her memoirs:

> 'All places rang with the fame of Mr Whitefield... I said, poor gentlemen! He is out of his mind; so foolish was I and ignorant! But he continued to blow the Gospel trumpet all round London.'[39]

Eventually curiosity made her want to go and hear him, but her husband refused to let her go. That may have been because the Common was hardly a salubrious place for a young mother, but Grace gives the impression it was more because Murray was opposed to anything that smacked of religious fanaticism.

After a couple of weeks Murray left to resume his work at sea and almost immediately afterwards their infant daughter Susanna fell ill and died. Grace became deeply depressed:

> 'As I looked at her laid out upon the table, thoughts of death seized strongly upon me. This was followed by a strange lowness of spirits, without any intermission. Everything looked black and gloomy. I could take pleasure in nothing. Nor could any company divert me.... [Despite all my sister] could say or do, my

---

38 Extracts from GW's Journal 8 and 12 May 1739. Most historians argue he over-estimated the size of the crowds and it has been suggested his figures can be halved – even so these were enormous gatherings.
39 GBM pg 4

heaviness increased more and more.' [40]

She felt such an aching void that she did not know what to do:

'[I] said to my sister, 'I don't know what is the matter with me, but I think it is my soul'. She replied, 'Your soul, child! You are good enough for yourself and me too'. Poor creature! She was as ignorant as myself... The Lord had made the wound, and no earthly balm could cure it.' [41]

A young person in their neighbourhood called Marie Price encouraged Grace to ignore her husband's command and to accompany her to hear Whitefield preach at Blackheath, which was another of the open-air venues being used by him. It was a common not far from Greenwich and much used as a meeting place, although, like Kennington, it had a bad reputation. Whitefield had commenced preaching regularly there in June. In her desperation Grace agreed to go. She says they could hear people singing hymns before they reached the place where Whitefield was scheduled to preach and 'the very sound set all my passions afloat':

'My heart was melted down as soon as I heard them, and I felt a sweetness I had never felt before. I looked up and wondered where I was. When Mr Whitefield came I thought there was something in his look which I had never seen. He preached on John 3 v. 8. I listened and liked all I heard.... I found my heart fully drawn towards God, and I began to seek him with all my strength.' [42]

40 JWLL pg 20
41 GBM pg 5
42 JWLL pg 20-21.

The text Whitefield used was 'Verily, verily, I say unto thee, except a man be born again, he cannot see the Kingdom of Heaven'. In her old age Grace was to write:

> 'The unregenerate heart is a cage of unclean birds; all manner of abominations dwell there. It is one thing, however, to say thus, and another to feel it so. It is one thing to say I am a sinner, and another to feel myself under the wrath and curse of God for my sins. Many will complain of themselves, and say, oh, I am very sinful, my heart is wicked, etc, but still they go on to sin, and rest content... If they felt what they say, they could not stop there.' [43]

Grace, acutely aware of her own failings, struggled with the concept of what it meant to be born again. She therefore went to hear Whitefield three more times before he left London on 13 August to sail back to America. She still could not understand all that he said, but the thought of losing his guidance flung her once more into a state of depression. She says she 'wept much in secret'.[44] To her sister's alarm Grace began spending more and more time in the graveyard where her little child was buried. In a desperate attempt to lighten her mood, her sister arranged for her to attend a dance. Grace says the impact was not what had been intended:

> 'No sooner did I rise to dance with them than my knees smote together and all desire of all worldly diversions and pleasures was taken away from me in that moment.'[45]

On Sunday 9 September she opted to go with Marie Price and hear John Wesley preach in the Moorfields, although it was a place with

43 26 Aug 1792 GBM pg 37
44 JWLL pg 21
45 ibid

an even worse reputation than Kennington or Blackheath. The homes near and within Moorfields were all slums and it was known for its brothels and sporadic open-air markets and travelling shows. It had a reputation for harbouring highwaymen and other criminals. Wesley's account of his preaching on that occasion says there were ten thousand people present. Even if he exaggerated, it must have been an awesome event. Grace wrote afterwards:

'When Mr Wesley stood up, and looked round on the congregation, I fixed my eyes upon him and felt an inexpressible conviction that he was sent by God. And when he spoke those words, 'Except a man be born again, he cannot see the Kingdom of God', they went through me like a dart, and I cried out, 'Alas! What shall I do? How shall I be born again?'[46]

John Wesley's preaching about new birth differed in one very important respect from that of Whitefield, who was a Calvinist. John proclaimed that salvation was not just for a preordained select few. It was open to all, even the most worthless of sinners, through the grace of God. For the first time Grace felt that it might be possible for her to be a recipient of God's forgiveness and she literally trembled:

'[He said] 'Is there anyone here that has a true desire to be saved?' My heart replied, 'Yes, I have.' He added, 'My soul for thine, if thou continue laying at the feet of Jesus.' On this word I took hold; for I was like a person drowning who would catch hold of anything to save his life'.[47]

Marie Price told her that what she was experiencing was God's

46 JWLL pg 22
47 GBM pg 7

hammer of love striking at her heart and she suggested that she should begin attending a religious society that met on Wednesday evenings in Fetter Lane. This society, which owed much to the influence of the Moravian Church, was at the heart of a network of about thirty other religious societies.[48] Most met on a weekly basis either in a hired room or in a tavern so that their members could encourage each other's faith. Members would sing a psalm or two, study a chosen religious book, and pray together. All of these societies had been encouraged by Whitefield's preaching and the one in Fetter Lane was where John and Charles Wesley were members.

Thanks to the Moravians, the society had become what one historian has described as 'a religious pollen factory'[49], attracting a cross section of the various religious groups functioning in the capital, including not only German Moravians and English Calvinists but also French Huguenots. Not surprisingly orthodox clergy judged it as politically suspect and condemned its strange mixture of religious ecumenism and social egalitarianism. Grace says she did have a momentary panic as to whether she should be going to it and listening to men like Whitefield and Wesley, but, after she had re-read certain passages of the Bible, her doubts fell away. She soon became a committed adherent:

'I comprehended all that I heard, as much as if I had studied it several years. And from this time I omitted no opportunity of attending the preaching in every place.'

She was therefore horrified when it was announced at a society

---

48 The Moravian Church was a relatively new one, although it traced its beginnings back to Jan Hus, the fifteenth-century Czech Protestant reformer. It was sending missionaries to America and they stayed in London en route to travelling to the colonies there. It was a Moravian, Peter Bohler, who had been very instrumental in helping bring both John and Charles to a much stronger faith in 1738.

49 David Hempton, Methodism: Empire Of The Spirit, Yale Univ. Press, New Haven and London 2005 pg 14

meeting that this was to be the last time John Wesley would address them because he would shortly be leaving to return to Bristol. Having lost Whitefield, the thought of losing Wesley was too much for her. On the way home she collapsed:

'I felt as if my heart was bound round with an iron girdle. I knew myself to be a lost, dammed sinner without Christ, without faith, hanging over the mouth of Hell.... I could not speak or cry out, but only groan to God.... 'Why hast thou forsaken me?"[50]

She went to hear Wesley preach at Pankridge before his departure and was equally distraught. She could not eat or drink or sleep properly. However, a week after Wesley had left, she experienced a dramatic shift in her mood:

'I was sitting in my own house with Marie Price reading the fifth chapter of Romans, when, in a moment, all things became new. I seemed to have new eyes and a new understanding. I saw all I read in a new light. My burden dropped off. My soul was in peace.... My tears were all gone. And I said to her, 'Now I know God is my God and he has forgiven me my sins.' [51]

Assured she was 'a child of God'[52] Grace started telling anyone she met, whether rich or poor, to seek their salvation. This included urging the local prostitutes in Sailortown to turn to God. John Wesley later wrote of this time in her life:

'She heard: pure love her soul o'erflow'd

50 JWLL pg 23-4

51 JWLL pg 24. The Romans chapter speaks of being saved through Christ's sacrificial death even though humanity is sinful.

52 GBM pg 9

Sorrow and sighing fled away:
With sacred zeal her spirit glow'd:
Panting His every word to obey,
Her faith by plenteous fruit she shew'd,
And all her works were wrought in God.'[53]

Many judged that Grace had become a religious fanatic. This was not surprising. Apart from her evangelical undertakings, Grace would sometimes sit in a room of people and be totally oblivious of all that was being said to her because she was so engrossed in religious meditation. She says that her sister told her that, whereas once she had been able to take pleasure in seeing Grace in the company of others, now 'she hated to see me there, [because] I looked so much like a fool'[54] and desired 'I would keep my madness to myself, and not make her mad too.'[55] Grace ignored such criticism of her behaviour. She drew strength from how God used her to help a dying man who was terrified that he was destined for Hell. She was able to give him the confidence to believe that he could be forgiven and so he died in peace, singing praises to God. Nevertheless, it was not long before Grace's own sense of having obtained forgiveness came to an end:

'I went on in great joy for four months: then pride crept in and I thought the work was finished when it was but just begun... and in a little time fell into doubts and fears whether my sins were really forgiven me, till I plunged myself into the depths of misery. I could not pray; neither had I any desire to do it, or to read or hear the word. My soul was like the troubled sea. Then did I see my own evil heart, my cursed devilish nature and feel my helplessness that I could not so much as think a good

53 JW's Poem on Grace Murray.
54 GBM pg 9
55 JWLL pg 25

thought. My love was turned into hatred, passion, envy, etc. I felt a thousand hells my due and cried out in anguish of spirit, 'Save me, Lord, or I perish.'[56]

This may sound an overly dramatic response but it should be put within the context of what John Wesley was encouraging her to do. As one recent historian has written: 'Talking about one's sins was fundamental to early Methodist culture.'[57] Wesley expected groups to ask each other probing questions about what they had said, done, and thought, and he urged individuals to confess how they had been tempted and what sins they had committed. For someone like Grace, who was prone to be highly self-critical, this was a recipe for potential disaster. Far from strengthening her faith, it began to make her feel she must have none. It was a meeting with Charles Wesley in the April of 1740 that helped her to start emerging from her resulting despair. He encouraged her to join the new 'United Society' that he and his brother had recently opened in the Foundery, a derelict former factory for the casting of cannons in Windmill Street, near Finsbury Square.[58]

By this stage the Wesleys had largely been pushed out of the Fetter Lane Society because the Moravians disapproved of John's constant emphasis on striving for Christian perfection. They thought it encouraged people to believe they could earn their salvation. They also hated John's acceptance of highly emotional behaviour. The aims of the new society were simple ones – to provide a place where people could gather together to pray and seek 'the power of godliness', 'receive the word of exhortation', 'watch over one another

---

56 GM letter to CW May 1740 cited in W. Stamp, The Orphan House of Wesley, J. Mason 1863 pg 45

57 M.G. Anderson, Imagining Methodism in Eighteenth-Century Britain, John Hopkins Univ. Press 2012 pg 81

58 Windmill Street later became known as Tabernacle Street. The building had been wrecked by an explosion in 1716 and was no more than 'a vast, uncouth heap of ruins' when Wesley purchased it.

in love', and 'help each other to work out their salvation'.[59] It was also a place where the brothers intended to distance themselves from both Moravian and Calvinist thinking and develop a better control over what people believed theologically. The Foundery was modelled largely on the two bases that the Wesleys had already created for their work in and around Bristol – the New Room and the preaching house and school in Kingswood. The main Foundery building could cater for 1,500 people and it also had a smaller meeting room. Over the next few years it was to develop other facilities and become the main base for Methodist work in London.

Brought up within the Anglican Church, Grace had been taught that women should always look for religious guidance to an ordained minister. She called Charles Wesley her 'reverend Father in God'. She was later to say that having to face his piercing look was something she never forgot and that she could never cease being grateful enough for the help that he gave her. Charles does not mention Grace by name but he does provide an account of one of the meetings he ran for women at the Foundery:

'I began praying and we were all overwhelmed. I spoke largely of their being brought into the wilderness, of their folly and ingratitude... My love and sorrow ran through them all.... [I] warned them against disputing... Jane Jackson and others witnessed what God had done for their souls through our ministry. If Christ be not with us, who hath begotten these? His power overshadowed us at this time. Therefore our heart danced for joy, and in our song did we praise him.'[60]

Nevertheless, overcoming her sense of failure did not prove easy

---

59 The Nature, Design and General Rules of the United Societies May 1743, Wesley's Works (1872 edition) Vol VIII pg 269

60 8 April 1740 CWJ Vol 1 pg 237

for Grace. She says that for a month she alternated between bouts of faith and times when she was 'ready to disbelieve everything in Scriptures' to the point of almost becoming an atheist.[61] It was eventually through the medium of prayer that her doubts about her chances of salvation were answered in May 1740:

'Whether I was in the body or out of the body I know not, but I saw what no human tongue can express... concerning the glory of the Divine Persons in the Godhead. I was also made sensible that God the Father accepted me in His Son as if I had not committed one sin; and that the righteousness of the Lord Jesus Christ was imputed to me for justification, with all that He purchased by His life and death; and at the same time these words were applied to my soul with the greatest power: 'Peace I leave with thee; my peace I give unto thee'. The [Holy] Spirit itself bore witness with my spirit that I was a child of God.'[62]

She says she was filled 'with such a reverential love as it had not entered my heart to conceive' and that the impact of this vision stayed with her for months: 'This glorious sight was always before my eyes... I walked as on the clouds and trod both sin and temptation under foot.' [63]

Her resulting renewed religious enthusiasm led all her former friends to abandon her. Some modern writers have not always looked on her transformation with any kinder an eye. It has been suggested that this and subsequent mood swings arose from the fact she suffered from manic depression.[64] It is claimed that is why one of her sons later wrote that there were occasions when the Devil

61 GBM pg15-16
62 GBM pg 8-9
63 JWLL pg 27
64 S.R. Valentine, John Bennet and the Origins of Methodism, Scarecrow Press 1997 g 204

threatened to devour his mother 'with all the fury of a roaring lion'.[65] It is certainly true that throughout her memoirs Grace often describes having bouts of depression and sometimes juxtaposes those with moments of elation. It is also fair to say that there are other strange aspects to her behaviour – she talks of hearing voices, having premonitions, suffering terrible nightmares, and having daylight visions. Her writing is full of references to emotional behaviour: fainting, giddiness, depression, exaltation, bouts of lethargy, and so on. While the diagnosis of manic depression cannot be ruled out, it probably stems largely from the difficulty we have in the twenty-first century of grasping just how much a person in the eighteenth century could fear eternal damnation – and the emotional impact of that. Virtually all eighteenth-century evangelicals were prone to make stark, dramatic and often over-exaggerated statements when describing the ups and downs of their faith. Experiencing dreams and nightmares, premonitions and visions, regular attacks by the Devil and dark nights of the soul – these were all part and parcel of what was expected. Neither John nor Charles Wesley ever suggested that anything about Grace's behaviour was strange.

The reason for Alexander Murray's absence during the time that Grace became a member of first the Fetter Lane Society and then of the United Society at the Foundery was that he had been taken a prisoner of war. In October 1739 Britain had declared war on Spain because it was keen to break the virtual monopoly that Spain enjoyed on trade with South America and to curtail its trade in the Caribbean and elsewhere. The pretext for the war was that back in 1731 some Spanish coast guards in Florida had boarded a British ship, claiming it was engaged in smuggling. They had punished its captain, Robert Jenkins, by cutting off his left ear. This story was resurrected along with other tales of the Spanish confiscating

65 GBM pg 15

the goods on British shipping and holding and torturing crews. Unfortunately the Royal Navy was not in a position to immediately protect its merchant shipping once war had been declared, and, as a consequence, many merchant ships were boarded by the Spaniards and forced to dock in Spanish ports, where their goods were taken as the spoils of war.[66] Murray's ship was one of those.

When Alexander Murray finally secured his release and returned to London, he was totally taken aback by Grace's religious fervour. Her first words to him were that he should cease swearing and turn to God for salvation. Understandably he sought to find out what had happened in his absence from Grace's relatives:

'After a while he walked to see my brother [in-law] and sister who told him, 'We are glad to see you, but we are sorry for you on account of your poor mad wife. She goes to hear those Methodists.'[67]

Murray was horrified and immediately banned her from going to any more Methodist meetings:

'He stamped and raved and swore, 'You shall leave them or me.' I answered, 'I love you above anyone on earth. But I will leave you and all that I have sooner than I will leave Christ.'[68]

In response he made clear to her that he had no objection to her attending a church or seeking to serve God, but he would not have the Methodists wreck the happy life they had enjoyed together.

66 The Navy's main initial focus was to send a fleet to the West Indies. An early victory – the fall of Porto Bello on the coast of Panama – was hailed by celebrations in London in the spring of 1740. These included the public debut of the song 'Rule Britannia'.

67 JWLL pg 28. 'Methodists' had become the word applied to all the followers of Whitefield and the Wesleys.

68 ibid

Grace says what made him particularly cross was that 'I would not be a party in such pleasures as I used to delight in'.[69] When she refused to accompany him to 'scenes of pleasure and vain delight' he consulted with his brother-in-law and the two men agreed that Grace should be locked up in a madhouse if she refused to renounce her links with Methodism. This threat failed to persuade Grace. She remained defiant, saying 'Put me into whatever place you please, the Lord will go with me'.[70] Fortunately for her, such was Murray's love for her that could not bring himself to have her locked away. Instead he tried using emotional blackmail, saying her behaviour was driving him back to sea and he would 'go as far as ship can sail'. To this she replied:

> 'I can not help it. I could lay down my life for you. But I cannot destroy my soul. If you are resolved to go, you must go. I give you up to God.'[71]

Murray then resorted to bribery, offering to give her whatever she wanted if she would just leave the Methodists. When this also failed, he confined her to the house and made sure none of her Methodist friends could visit her. Then, when he eventually let her go outside again, he warned her of the dire consequences she would face if she went to the Foundery. She ignored his threats and promptly went there. She says the society members greeted her with great joy. When she returned home she was understandably apprehensive but, to her surprise, her husband said nothing about her behaviour. Not long afterwards Grace was taken sick, almost certainly because she was pregnant again. She was confined to bed and it was feared her life was in danger. Alexander Murray wanted her to see a doctor but she

69 GBM pg 10
70 ibid
71 JWLL pg 29

insisted on seeing first some of her fellow Methodists. Initially he refused her request but then his love for her overcame his prejudice:

'He asked one day if I would have him read by me? I said 'With all my heart'. He read till the tears came down from his cheeks, and he said, 'Send for whom you have a mind'.[72]

Murray deliberately avoided meeting any of her Methodist visitors, but, when Grace recovered, he gave permission for her to go to the Foundery. One evening he noticed she was reading a copy of the published journal of George Whitefield and he began to read it. This proved a turning point:

'[He] said, 'I know God has forgiven me many and great sins, but I cannot forgive myself'. The tears started into his eyes and he said, 'If these good men talk so, what must I do, for I am a sinner indeed?' I clapped my hands and began praying earnestly for him. He went on, 'I think you are in the right. I fear I have been fighting against God. If it please God to raise you again, I will never hinder you more.' From this time on... he searched the Scriptures much, willingly heard me read and talk as I was able of the things of God... and desired nothing so much as to know Jesus Christ, and Him crucified'. [73]

When Murray returned to his ship he sent the pregnant Grace back to her parents' house in Newcastle so she could be fully looked after. By this time Methodism had made its first tentative entry into Newcastle. A small group of Methodists, perhaps no more than a dozen, were meeting for fellowship in a room in Lisle Street.

72 JWLL pg 30
73 JWLL pg 31

How this group came into being is not known but it may well have stemmed from a visit in 1740 of Westley Hall, the brother-in-law of the Wesleys. He was a clergyman who had belonged to the Holy Club that John and Charles had run in Oxford and he had promised to help initiate the religious revival. Charles Wesley was later to record that the memory of Hall's preaching was fondly remembered by some of the people in Newcastle. Grace's father had no desire for his daughter to continue her links to Methodism. She says that he initially thought, like her sister, that she was mad but gradually, just like her husband, he was won over to accepting her Methodism. In his case that was because he saw the positive changes it had wrought in her character. He admired his daughter's newfound truthfulness and sobriety.

In November Grace received a report from her sister that her husband had again been captured by the Spaniards but was returning home and that his ship was anchored in Yarmouth Roads awaiting a favourable wind. That month was very stormy and Grace had to calm her mother's fears that Alexander was likely to be drowned. Yarmouth Roads was a stretch of usually very safe water. According to Grace, God told her in her prayers that her husband was alright:

'It was clearly shown me he would return: and I said to my mother one morning, 'This day I should see my husband'. About four in the afternoon he knocked at the door. I dropped down but soon rose again and praised God.'[74]

Sadly Robert Norman was taken sick just three days later and, after a week's illness, he died. He was buried on 13 November in the graveyard of St Andrew's Church. After the funeral Grace and her husband returned to London and once again set up home in

74 JWLL pg 32

Stepney. Grace says that Alexander followed 'the home trade' so he could stay with her as much as possible during her pregnancy.[75] In early May 1741 she gave birth to a baby boy. Less than two days after the baby's birth Murray failed to return home. The mystery was solved when a neighbour brought the terrible news that he had been press-ganged and was on board a ship that was headed for Virginia. There was a particular need for more experienced sailors at this time because France had joined forces with the enemy Spain. This meant the Royal Navy was faced with having to escort merchant shipping across to America and to the West Indies and so protect them from attack. The only method they had of obtaining the necessary sailors was to press-gang men into service.

Grace went to see her husband in Deptford before the ship set sail. It was an emotional meeting. He confessed that he was a sinner and asked her if she would get her Methodist friends to pray for him. She wrote afterwards:

'I then found great power to speak to his heart. We wept much till we were forced to part... I gave him up to God without one discontented thought.'[76]

Their infant son was christened John on 17 June at St George in the East and she nicknamed him 'Jackey'.

By this stage John Wesley had appointed Grace as a band leader at the Foundery. Many of the members within religious societies chose to encourage each other by grouping into small bands of five or six people. It was customary for each band to be single-sex and for it to contain people who were similar in age or status (such as being unmarried, married or widowed). The concept of women

75 JWLL pg 33
76 JWLL pg 33-4

praying and talking together posed no challenge to the orthodoxy of the day as to what was and was not permissible for women to do. Nevertheless, becoming a band leader was for Grace and many other women a life-changing experience because it gave them an opportunity to voice their faith to like-minded women without that causing offence to the outside world. The Wesleys' emphasis on the importance of prayer and its often charismatic nature made it permissible for women to say public prayers in meetings, but any woman who went beyond that risked being accused of breaking the ban imposed by St Paul on females speaking in church.[77] However, within a band, this restriction did not apply and women could speak freely about their faith. This included not just giving personal testimony but engaging if they wished in formal discussion of spiritual issues. Some of the female band leaders, including Grace, saw nothing wrong in also 'expounding' – i.e. talking about a passage of scripture – although the Church frowned on this, judging it to be a form of preaching. Grace was to become one of the first female leaders to challenge the distinctions as to what a woman could and could not do.

Wesley also made Grace a visitor to the sick. In many ways this was far more demanding than being a band leader. It was not just about offering kindness , sympathy, and assistance to those who were ill. Sickness can predispose a person to think about what really matters and so the visitor's role was to make use of that and to encourage those they visited to think about their salvation. Even more importantly, it was also about trying to ensure that those who were dying received the opportunity to repent and seek God's forgiveness before they died. This meant that visitors had to be able to talk easily and comfortably about issues of faith and tackle often very difficult questions. They had to handle the anguish of those

---

77 1 Corinthians 14 v. 34 says: 'It is a shocking thing that a woman should address a congregation'.

who suffered and deal not only with their hopes and fears but also with the feelings of their families. Judging from the nursing role that John Wesley later asked Grace to play, he must have judged her role as a sick visitor to have been particularly effective. She was later to describe visiting the sick as her 'delight'.[78]

The months passed and in May 1742 Grace had a dream which convinced her that Alexander must have died at sea:

'I was one night just laid down when I felt a weight came upon my feet. I thought the cat had come upon me and strove to push her off. Presently I felt it rising higher and higher by my side till it seemed to lie by me at full length of a man. I felt an awe, but no fear... After a few minutes it rolled off and fell upon the ground. I fell asleep and dreamed I saw my husband lying in his coffin... When I waked I was convinced my husband was dead.'[79]

In October she was given hope that she was wrong. The wife of a ship's cook told Grace that she had just visited her husband on board 'The Prince Frederick', which had recently returned from America for refitting, and that she thought she had seen Alexander. This was not the ship onto which Murray had been press-ganged but Grace and her sister rushed to see if the report was true.[80] They were at once informed that he had died at sea. It is not clear how this information was known but there are two possibilities. The convoy ships sent to Virginia had sailed next to the West Indies to protect

78 GBM pg 14

79 JWLL pg 34 It has been argued that this dream 'condenses both her sexual and spiritual longings' and that the premonition 'seems to veil an unconscious wish for death, an unconscious longing for release from her sexual desire, and anger at her husband for leaving her with no way to fulfil those desires.' J.P. Briggs & J.Briggs, Unholy Desires, Inordinate Affections, Connecticut Review Spring 1991. I think this reads far too much into the text.

80 'The Prince Frederick had been relaunched in the spring of 1740 after a rebuild and joined a fleet under the command of Rear-Admiral Sir Challoner Ogle. It had taken part between March and May 1741 in the fighting around Cartagena de Indias on the coast of Colombia. Damaged, it had then gone for repairs to Jamaica.

merchant shipping travelling from America. Murray might have been reassigned to 'The Prince Frederick' in Jamaica and so served on that ship for a time. Alternatively Edward Boscawen, the captain of 'The Prince Frederick', might have picked up news of British losses either in the West Indies or when his ship passed through the Bay of Biscay on its way home.

The news of her husband's death, despite her earlier premonition, threw Grace into such a state of shock that initially she felt no reaction. It was only when she got back to her sister's house in Stepney that her loss sank home: 'I shrieked, 'What must I see him no more?'... and dropped down and lost my senses'.[81] Such was her subsequent suffering that Grace was later to say her mind was never quite the same again. It has been suggested that Grace's account of her intense love for her dead husband was deliberately conveyed to Wesley in a way that was designed to put John 'on notice about her strong sexual needs'[82], but that reads far more into the manuscript than is reasonable. Grace had deeply loved her husband and she simply saw no reason to disguise that fact from Wesley or anyone else.

Her mother suggested Grace should return to Newcastle with her infant son. Grace sought John Wesley's advice and he said she should go and that, as he was intending to visit Newcastle, he would meet up with her there. Grace set off for the north and the journey proved horrendous. A three-day storm so diverted the ship off its course that it ended up off the coast of Scotland and narrowly avoided crashing onto the rocks. Grace says her faith helped her remain calm, even though 'the ship was tossed mountain high' and she saw 'the wonders of the deep'.[83] A new and exciting chapter was about to open for the young widow.

81 JWLL pg 35
82 J.P. Briggs & J. Briggs, Unholy Desires, Inordinate Affections, Connecticut Review, Spring 1991
83 GBM pg 12

NEWCASTLE-UPON-TYNE, FROM NEW CHATHAM, GATESHEAD.

Newcastle-upon-Tyne (from print in the New Room)

John Wesley preaching at the Sandgate in Newcastle (from print in the New Room)

2

CLASS LEADER, PREACHER AND HOUSEKEEPER

John Wesley's interest in Newcastle had first been aroused in May 1742 when he had visited the north at the request of the Yorkshire stonemason John Nelson. He says in his journal that he was shocked by seeing and hearing so much 'drunkenness, cursing and swearing (even from the mouths of little children)' [84] and that he could see no evidence that the earlier visit by his brother-in-law, Westley Hall, had borne any fruit in the lifestyle of the people. John chose to preach in Sandgate, the most populous area of the city. It contained a vast number of narrow lanes all lined with overcrowded houses. He attracted large crowds – far larger than anything he had seen in Bristol or London. The few Methodists in the city begged him to stay but Wesley could not because of prior commitments. One of them, Christopher Hopper, subsequently commented: 'He made a short blaze, soon disappeared, and left us in great consternation.'[85]

It was left to Charles Wesley to devote time to preaching in Newcastle. He arrived some months later but there is a gap in his journal that prevents us having details about his visit. What we know

---

84 JWJ 27 May 1742
85 Cited in W. Stamp, The Orphan House of Wesley, J. Mason 1863 pg 4

from other sources is that he was accompanied by a man called Matthew Errington, who originated from Houghton-le-Spring, a small town about twenty miles from Newcastle. Errington had given up a good job in London in order to become a servant to the preachers at the Foundery, saying: 'I would rather be a doorkeeper in the house of God than to dwell in the tents of wickedness'.[86] His local knowledge made him an ideal companion. Charles' preaching proved most effective and about eight hundred people joined what became the first official Methodist society in the north. John Wesley returned to Newcastle on 13 November in order to build on his brother's success. He took up residence in a public house that was in the countryside outside Newcastle but only a mile from Sandgate. He met the members of the religious society that Charles had nurtured, and began public preaching the next day.

By 18 November Wesley was expressing his joy at the numbers attending his preaching but his frustration at how few were responding:

'The grace of God flows here with a wider stream than it did at first either at Bristol or Kingswood. But it does not sink so deep as it did there. Few are thoroughly convinced of sin, and scarce any witness that the Lamb of God has taken away their sins.'[87]

A week later he bemoaned that he saw 'none of that triumph of faith which has been so common in other places', but he praised 'the believers' for not letting this upset them.[88] The Methodists were still meeting in the room they had hired in Lisle Street and it was there that Grace Murray went on her arrival. She was more positive about

---

86 ibid pg 9. He later became a member of the staff at the Orphan House known for reproving sin and 'promoting brotherly love'.

87 JWJ 18 Nov 1742

88 JWJ 25 Nov 1742

what was happening:

> 'I found that Mr Wesley had been preaching both in the town
> and in the fields, and that people had flocked to hear the gospel;
> which caused my spirits to revive when I saw how the arm of
> the Lord was stretched out to save sinners in my native county.'[89]

According to Grace, she spent her time either listening to Wesley in
the house where he was staying or accompanying him to wherever
he was preaching. When John was undertaking work in Horsley, a
small village about ten miles west of Newcastle, he asked Grace to
stay on and follow up his preaching:

> 'He took me with him and left me there. I endeavoured to
> improve my time by speaking to everyone I could, either at
> Horsley or the neighbouring villages, as well as by praying with
> those of the Society.'[90]

Having a mother like Susanna Wesley had left John with a strong
predisposition towards using the talents of women to help create
a religious revival. He knew, for example, that she had drawn
a far larger congregation to her worship sessions in the family
home than attended his father's services in the parish church. This
predisposition had been reinforced by his reading of the book 'A
Serious Call', written by William Law, a Scottish theologian. Law
stated that women 'possessed a finer sense, a readier apprehension,
and gentler dispositions' than men and that they could probably
rise to 'greater heights of piety' than most men if they were suitably

89 GBM pg 13
90 JWLL pg 36-7

educated.[91] Wesley therefore saw nothing wrong in encouraging women to speak about their faith within the context of a Methodist society, although he accepted that, because of the ban imposed by St Paul, they should not speak within a church service. Critical to his use of women was that, alongside the voluntary bands, John had initiated, first at the New Room in Bristol and then subsequently in all his societies, a mandatory system of 'classes'. These were groups of about a dozen or so men and women who lived near each other. He chose women as well as men to lead these.

The challenges facing a class leader were far greater than those of a band leader. Bands tended to be like-minded friends choosing to support each other but those in a class often were very varied not only in their background and education but also in terms of their level of Christian understanding and experience. It was the class leader's role to deepen the faith of the members in his or her class and to ensure they tried to live truly Christian lives – and to recommend an end to their membership if they failed to do that. Grace and many other women found the role of class leader difficult but, at the same time, they usually felt it was very rewarding. This was well expressed by a leader called Margaret Davison:

'O how sweet it is… Christians meet in the house of prayer and are made joyful therein. They praise the majesty of heaven, and fall down before him in sacred devotion, freely and sweetly telling to one another what he has done for their souls and cordially agreeing in thanksgiving or prayer for each other. This is, indeed, the communion of saints.'[92]

91 For more on this see chapter on Methodists in Christine l. Krueger, The Reader's Repentance: Women Preachers, Women Writers, and Nineteenth-Century Social Discourse, Univ. of Chicago Press 1992

92 E. Smyth (edit.) The Extraordinary Life and Experience of Margaret Davison as dictated by herself, Dublin 1882 pg 63

The success of female class leaders encouraged societies to recognise that some women were well suited to 'exhort' at their meetings, even if they were not eligible because of their sex to become preachers.[93] What is unusual here is that John was requesting that Grace should not confine her public role to the society to which she belonged. She is therefore one of the first two Methodist women whom we know to have been authorised to a wider exhorting role.[94] Although she primarily addressed female bands within the societies she visited, it is clear that she also sometimes spoke to their classes and therefore to men as well. Moreover, like any male preacher, she did not confine her role to praying or speaking with bands and classes. Much of her time was spent holding more intimate conversations with individuals and families. In this context it is worth quoting what a later female preacher, Sarah Crosby, wrote:

'The greatest means of increasing Christian affection is close conversation concerning the work of God on our souls; speaking without reserve our trials, temptations, comforts and accordingly pleading with God.'[95]

Grace was wary of talking too much because she felt that it was often more vital to listen to people, but she was very comfortable about sharing her own Christian experience when that was required.[96] It is likely that her awareness of her own frailties was a strength rather than a weakness in that process. Of this time in her life she later wrote:

93 Wesley first drew up the distinction between 'exhorting' and 'preaching' in 1739 when he used it as an excuse to let his helper John Cennick preach. He told his fellow clergy, who were refusing to accept that a layman had any authority to preach, that Cennick was not preaching but merely exhorting and defined this as giving his personal testimony and speaking briefly to encourage people.

94 The other one was Sarah Perrin, who became housekeeper at the New Room in Bristol.

95 Letter To JW 25 April 1758 published in Arminian Magazine 1781 Vol IV pg 667

96 She said on one occasion: 'We are bidden to be swift to hear and slow to speak'.

'I had a settled peace, a full confidence in God, a burning zeal for his glory, and a vehement desire to spend and be spent for all men.'[97]

Her growing reputation as a fine exhorter led to her receiving invitations to speak. An example of that is the request she received from the Methodist society at Tanfield Lea, a small village about seven miles south-west of Newcasle. That she had influence is borne out by the fact she was the person responsible for encouraging one of the society members at Horsley, John Downes, to commence preaching. She says 'he found no want of words' and her judgement was good because Wesley was to come to view Downes as one of the most outstanding men of his generation.[98] There can be little doubt that Grace's achievements confirmed John's view that women could play their part in creating a religious revival. When he set in motion the creation of a permanent base for future work in Newcastle, he saw Grace as a potential key player.

Wesley wanted to create an equivalent building in Newcastle to the New Room in Bristol and the Foundery in London. On 8 December he acquired a piece of land outside the Pilgrim-Street Gate from a merchant called Stephenson. It was a good site because it was on the highest ground and therefore overlooked the whole city. The first stone for what soon became known as 'the Orphan House' was laid twelve days later. The name came from the fact that Wesley envisaged that one of the uses for the new building would be to educate poor children and he had in mind as a possible

97 JWLL pg 38

98 JWLL pg 37. Downes became an itinerant preacher and accompanied John Wesley and John Nelson on a tour of Cornwall in 1744. He was one of the four lay preachers to attend the first Methodist Conference that year. He was later press ganged into the army but, after his release, returned to preaching. In 1751 he gave up itinerant preaching in order to take charge of Methodist printing operations, but remained an important preacher in London until he died after collapsing in the pulpit of the West Street Chapel in 1774.

model an institution that he had seen in Halle in Germany called the Orphan-House. Many thought the scheme would not come to fruition because it was estimated that £700 would have to be raised to build what he wanted, but Wesley was confident God would ensure the funds were found. In sharp contrast to the hostility that Wesley usually faced from the clergy, it appears the new building had the support of Thomas Turner, the vicar of St Nicholas' Church. Apparently he had a dream in which he saw 'angels ascending and descending on a ladder on that very spot' and took this as a sign it would be a place where many were awakened to their salvation. [99]

Wesley appointed Grace to be the leader of a number of the female bands and the mixed-sex classes. He also asked her to come and stay in his lodgings so she could nurse the young Cornish preacher, Thomas Meyrick, who had accompanied him to Newcastle. Meyrick had fallen ill with such a severe cold that it was thought he was going to die. The preacher recovered under her care but not all the women in the society approved of Grace sharing a house with Wesley. It was the first indicator of the female jealousy that was subsequently to cause her so many problems. That she and Wesley had become very friendly is borne out by the fact he suggested that she might like to return with him to London and take up residence with him at the Foundery. Grace instantly agreed to this and set about purchasing her passage on a ship. If one believes John's account, she was already in love with him at this stage although she did not voice that. It is more likely that she simply worshipped him. There were also other reasons why a return to London was attractive to her. It was a far more exciting city and very much at the centre of the religious revival, and she was anxious to leave Newcastle because she was being pressurised by her mother to marry a man called John Brydon, whom she had been instrumental in converting. He had

99 W. Stamp, The Orphan House of Wesley, John Mason 1863 pg 20

misconstrued her interest in his spiritual welfare as meaning she must love him and become a nuisance.

Some of the women who were jealous of Grace informed Wesley about Brydon, insinuating that Grace was a most inappropriate choice as his companion because of her flirtatious behaviour. They also alleged that she had been going around making inappropriate comments about one of the female society members. When John informed Grace of the charges brought against her, she held a meeting with the women and they retracted their allegations. She also made clear to John that she did not love Brydon and that her grief over her dead husband was far too great for her to be contemplating a remarriage. Nevertheless, the idea of her going to London was dropped, probably because John Wesley had no desire to risk fuelling rumours about his own relationship with Grace. He advised her to go into the countryside and not tell Brydon where she was. She says she went back to living at her mother's house 'and came no more to Mr Wesley's'.[100]

On 30 December Wesley left Newcastle, instructing Grace to continue her work in the surrounding villages but without letting him know what she was doing. This was probably his way of saying that he could not officially authorise her to preach but he was happy for her to exhort as much as she liked. Judging from some of Wesley's later correspondence with women who preached, he always tried to cloak their activity under the guise they were only giving personal testimony and short exhortations. For example, in 1761 a class leader called Sarah Crosby proved so effective that her class group expanded into a meeting of over two hundred people. He told her:

'You lay me under a great difficulty. The Methodists do not allow of female preachers; neither do I take upon me any such

100 JWLL pg 39

character. But I will nakedly tell you what is in my heart... I do not see that you have broken any law.'[101]

And he subsequently advised her:

'In public you may properly enough intermix short exhortations with prayer; but keep as far from what is called preaching as you can: therefore never take a text; never speak in a continued discourse without some break, about four or five minutes. Tell the people, 'We shall have another *prayer meeting* at such a time and place.'[102]

Only in the 1770s and 1780s did Wesley commence abandoning such pretences. He then said that some women had an extraordinary call from God to preach and they were therefore exceptions to the Pauline ban – and he quoted Biblical examples to prove that this was acceptable – notably the prophetesses in the Old Testament and the role of Priscilla as described in chapter 18 of the Acts of the Apostles.

John Wesley did not return to Newcastle until 19 February 1743. According to his journal, the main society had by then lost seventy-six members. Most of these had gone either because of the opposition they had faced from employers or parents or partners or clergy or because of their dislike at being publicly ridiculed. In addition sixty-four members had been expelled for bad behaviour, which ranged from cursing and swearing and getting drunk to 'habitual, wiful lying', railing and evil-speaking', and 'lightness and carelessness'.[103] Despite this, the Newcastle society still numbered over eight hundred members. Enough work had taken place on the Orphan House for him to preach an opening sermon in its 'shell'

101 J. Telford, Letters of JW, Epworth 1931 Vol IV pg 133
102 ibid Vol V pg 130. Emphasis is that of Wesley.
103 JWJ 8 March 1743

on 25 March.[104] The new building had three floors. At ground level was a large preaching room designed so that the male members could sit on one side and the female members on the other with seats for strangers in the middle. Under the elevated pulpit was a door that led into a garden at the rear of the building. On the middle floor there was a large society meeting room with four classrooms either side of it. On the top floor there were ten small rooms to provide accommodation for visiting preachers and facilities for a housekeeper. There was a small additional garret room on the roof and this was later known as 'Mr Wesley's study'.

He published a pamphlet outlining 'the nature, design, and general rules of the 'United Societies' that he had created in Bristol, Kingswood, London and Newcastle. It said the only condition for membership was a desire to be saved from your sin and evidence that you were serious about that. The latter meant 'avoiding evil in every kind', whether that was 'taking the name of God in vain' or engaging in bad behaviour, such as getting drunk, singing bawdy songs, gossiping, or being guilty of 'needless self-indulgence'. It also meant showing a willingness to do good 'of every possible sort and, as far as possible, to all men... by giving food to the hungry, by clothing the naked, by visiting or helping them that are sick or in prison... [and] by instructing, reproving or exhorting all we have any intercourse with'. Members were also expected to participate in 'all the ordinances of God'. That included attending regular public worship and services of holy communion, as well as engaging in regular private prayer, Bible study, and fasting. [105]

Wesley worked in the city and surrounding region until 7 April. During that he must have decided that he had been wrong to rescind his offer of letting Grace work at the Foundery because she

104 JWJ 25 March 1743

105 The Nature, Design and General Rules of the United Societies May 1743, Wesley's Works (1872 edition) Vol VIII pg 270-1

took passage on a ship for London. She says that by this stage she had received assurance from God that she would be among those who were saved. It is not clear whether Jackey accompanied her or whether he was looked after by her mother in Newcastle. If Grace hoped that a return to London would entail her working more closely with John and Charles Wesley she was soon disappointed. Both men were now fully itinerant. Over the next seven months John was only in London for about ten weeks and Charles for about eight. It must have been particularly strange for Grace to be in London on those occasions when the brothers were in Newcastle.[106] By late October, when Wesley was heading for Newcastle again, it was agreed that Grace should return there and act as an assistant to Mrs Jackson, the housekeeper at the Orphan House.

In her account of her life Grace says 'I now gave myself up altogether to the service of the Church'.[107] She was playing a variety of roles. Within the city she was assistant housekeeper at the Orphan House and the leader of a significant number of bands and classes, as well as being assigned to help and challenge those who were ill. Outside the city she was continued to travel around the surrounding villages, encouraging the membership of the scattered rural Methodist societies. She had also become a visitor to 'the backsliders'. Wesley appears to have thought that some of his female class leaders – Grace being one – were particularly effective at dealing with those who were not living the lifestyle Christ required. Her account reflects all these roles :

'I had full a hundred in classes, whom I met in two separate meetings, and a band for each day of the week. I likewise visited the sick and backsliders, which was my pleasant meat. The work

106 Charles was based in the Newcastle area from 31 May to 19 June and John from 27 July to 18 August.
107 JWLL pg 40

of God was my delight; and when I was not employed in it, I seemed out of my element. We also had several societies in the country, which I regularly visited; meeting the women in the day time, and in the evening the whole society. And oh! what pourings out of the Spirit have I seen at these times! It warms my heart now while I relate it. I doubt not but I shall meet some of those precious souls, amongst whom I was so often refreshed in prayer, to sing the high praises of God and the Lamb for ever!' [108]

To undertake her role more effectively, Grace became a proficient rider and it appears that over the years her equestrian skill was to become a matter of some notoriety. The following account, for example, describes her mastery over her horse:

'Her horse stood waiting. She came out. A glance of her eye quickly told her all was right. No man might touch, even to help her, for she was on God's errand: so she laid her hand upon the conscious beast and it knelt to receive her. She sprang lightly into the saddle, waved her arm, and, as in a moment, was out of sight.' [109]

There were only two things that Grace found difficult to handle. One was the continued opposition she faced from some of the female members of the society.[110] The other was that her former suitor, John Brydon, had ceased attending society meetings after having married someone else. Watching a man whom she had saved become 'light and careless' made her fear that her rejection of him had caused his

---

108 GBM pg 13-14

109 Cited in Life of Jabez Bunting D.D. with notices of contemporary persons and events by his son Thomas Percival Bunting, Longmans 1859 Vol 1 pg 5. From a report given by Samuel Birks.

110 Grace particularly mentions a 'Sister Jackson'.

soul to be lost and that 'his blood would be upon my head.'[111] Her fear that she might therefore be numbered among the damned and not the saved was made far worse by listening to the lay preacher Thomas Maxfield when he visited Newcastle. Coming from a Calvinist background, Maxfield thought God had only chosen a few people for salvation and he had a propensity to declare that anyone unable to claim perfection was clearly not saved. For someone like Grace, who tended to be highly critical of her failings, this was disastrous. She convinced herself that, imperfect as she was, she must still be damned in God's eyes.

Throughout 1744 her state of depression grew ever worse as she increasingly feared she must be one of those people whom God had preordained to face eternal damnation:

'One day as I was walking over the Croft to meet my class I felt a cloud fall... on my body as well as my soul. A horrible darkness overwhelmed me.... I cried out aloud, 'If thou be a God, save me!' But there was no answer. When I came to a stile I was violently tempted to throw myself down and dash my brains out.... I thought I had sinned so that God had quite forgotten me and given me up into the devil's hands.... I saw nothing but Hell before my eyes. I had no hope of escaping... I felt myself utterly banished from God... I had no spark of hope left, and saw nothing before me but the blackness of darkness for ever. I wished I had never been born.... I felt as if one had begun at the crown of my head and flayed off my skin, yea my flesh and all, to the very soles of my feet.'[112]

Grace did not confess her spiritual fears to John Wesley when he

111 JWLL pg 41
112 JWLL pg 42 and 44-5

arrived in Newcastle on 21 May 1744 or at any time during his stay, which lasted until 11 June. Yet page after page of her memoirs recounts her mounting misery because she had 'no sight of God, no peace, no hope'[113] and 'the more I reasoned the more confused I was'.[114] She began to question whether Jesus was just a good man rather than being the Son of God and she says she suffered 'a thousand other blasphemous imaginations'.[115] By the autumn her state of mind had led to a serious decline in her physical as well as her mental health. She was not eating properly because she was over-fasting in an attempt to bring herself closer to God, and she was not sleeping properly because her nights were 'scared with dreams and terrified with visions'.[116] Her friends, seeing her become like a walking skeleton, prayed for her physical recovery, unaware of the spiritual torment that lay behind it. Yet still she said nothing to anyone about her fear that she had damned herself in the sight of God. Instead she desperately tried to remain outwardly cheerful to the members of her bands and her classes. Giving personal testimony was an essential part of a leader's duties and she says 'it was truly hard work to encourage others in the very things wherein I myself was so much discouraged'.[117] Despite this, she felt she could not abandon her role:

> 'I did not dare to forsake those who were commit[ed] to my charge; neither to stay away either from the morning or the evening preaching. I likewise visited the sick, though I was myself shrunk almost into a skeleton. So many used to ask me Why I came out? and told me I was fitter to be in bed than

113 JWLL pg 48
114 JWLL pg 43
115 JWLL pg 47
116 JWLL pg 49
117 GBM pg 17

anywhere else.'[118]

At her lowest she contemplated whether, if she was preordained for damnation, she might just as well become an atheist. John Wesley later wrote of her time of 'Great Trial' (as she called it):

> 'Torn by the dogs of Hell she lay;
> By fear and sin encompast round.
> Anguish and pain and huge dismay,
> Till the loud, bitter cry outbroke,
> 'My God, why hast thou me forsook?'[119]

Grace did not confide the reason for her ill health to Charles Wesley, when he was based in the Newcastle area from 30 October to 14 December. This may have partly been because Charles was facing a variety of other pressures. In his journal he says the society in Newcastle was in poor shape and he had to criticise its members for their 'slackness and offences of various kinds'.[120] He spent some of his time purging the classes, taking away the membership of many. At the same time he had to deal with false allegations from two women that he was guilty of sexual misconduct. Charles, of course, believed in salvation for all and he did not think being saved made you perfect – that was something that only happened after you died. His preaching therefore made Grace question whether her fear that she had eternally damned herself by rejecting Brydon was justified. After one sermon in particular she says she went home 'rejoicing in hope' that God might love her despite her sinfulness.[121] However, her deep sense of her own failings meant this respite proved short-lived.

118 JWLL pg 47
119 JW's Poem on Grace Murray
120 CWJ 6 Nov 1744
121 JWLL pg 51 Grace says this was in 1745 but Charles was not in Newcastle that year. It was 1744.

She says the Devil suggested to her 'what pride and presumption it was for such a sinner as me to hope for mercy'. [122]

This did not prevent her being moved by Charles' farewell sermon, which she says proved very prophetic about the problems the city was about to face during the Jacobite rebellion of 1745:

'He said, 'If I am a messenger of God to preach the Gospel unto you, mark what I say, before you see my face again, you will have the man on the red horse, and the man on the pale horse.' When he spoke these words, the whole auditory trembled. I myself was there, and felt the mighty power of God. And it was not long ere we experienced the truth of his message: we had both war and death in abundance.'[123]

It was during the Christmas of 1744 that Grace finally confided all of her fears and feelings about being damned to someone. She spoke to the lay preacher William Briggs, who had come from London to take over from Charles:

'We had much conversation together. I opened my whole heart to him, not willingly keeping back anything. The more we conversed, the more my mind was eased. My doubt concerning the sins of John Brydon being imputed to me was now removed and the horrible dread was taken away.' [124]

Then in his early twenties, Briggs was a very educated man and the son of Henry Briggs, chaplain to King George II. He seems to have gone out of his way to talk with those who were worried about their faith. He wrote to John Wesley:

122 ibid
123 This is a recollection that is given in Grace's diary on 12 Nov 1795 GBM pg 58
124 JWLL pg 50

'I have… had close conversation with thirty-six of the women and nine of the young men here. Such a company of earnest souls I hardly ever met with together. One and all seem to have freedom from all outward sin, and are greatly desirous of being delivered entirely from sin. Most of them are truly blessed mourners and hungerers and thirsters after spiritual life and power, and in much misery without it; and seem resolutely bent to forsake all other comforts to enjoy the abiding Spirit of Christ dwelling in them… All (except about three or four) opened their hearts to me… And in great simplicity told me all their troubles. And nothing seems so grievous to them as the evil of their own heart, their unfaithfulness to the grace given, and their want of love to God. I was amazed that people whom I had never met before should be so wonderfully plain and open to me, a stranger.'[125]

One can see why Grace chose to go to him for guidance and she accepted his authoritative response that God loved her despite her failings.[126] Almost sixty years later, when her son edited her account of this time in his mother's life, he wrote not only of what had led to her depression but also its outcome, which was that Grace remained throughout her life very sympathetic to those troubled with doubts and fears:

'What she alludes to… as her Great Trial was such a scene of deep spiritual conflict, almost bordering on despair; into which she was brought by indulging in high-wrought speculative inquiries, and following a train of sceptical suggestions, till her

125 28 Dec 1744 to JW in Arminian Magazine 1778 pg 232-3

126 Briggs later married the daughter of one of the Wesleys' closest friends, Vincent Perronet, and Wesley gave him power of attorney to manage some of the activities of the Foundery, including its printing operations, in the 1750s. By that stage Briggs had ceased itinerancy and acquired a role working in the government's Ordnance Office.

mind was enveloped in darkness, and deprived of all sensible comfort. This she considered, in more advanced life, as permitted of God, to correct the bad effect of those undue caresses she met with among the societies; to humble her, and to make her know what was in her heart; as well as to teach her to sympathise with, and comfort, the souls of the distressed; for which, by painful experience, she was eminently qualified.'[127]

In the spring of 1745 Newcastle was caught up in the mounting national fear that there was going to be a Jacobite invasion. Grace totally accepted the Wesleys' view that what was happening was God's punishment 'on a people laden with iniquities' and that, unless the nation turned back to God, 'the Papists were just going to swallow us up.'[128] This made the return of John Wesley on 23 February particularly welcome. John had ridden through an appalling snowstorm to get to the Orphan House and the weather remained very bad. He therefore spent the first few days in individual meetings with his followers. As soon as he felt it was possible, John embarked on a preaching tour of the villages outside Newcastle and he asked Grace to accompany him. She agreed and proved an effective companion. She says: 'I never wanted power from God to pray with, and labour among, the people'.[129] Wesley had a reputation for exhausting those who travelled with him and that may explain why she fell sick almost immediately afterwards. However, for her the importance of the tour was that it confirmed in her own mind that Briggs had been right and that, despite all her failings, God loved her and wanted to use her:

'I had a full and clear sense of the pardoning love of God, and I

127 GBM pg 15
128 JWLL pg 50-51
129 JWLL pg 51

knew my soul was set at liberty, and that Satan was departed from me. I saw all I had suffered had been for good....[and realised] God had been walking.... [with me]when I went through the fires.'[130]

She therefore made no complaint about her illness: 'Pain was now nothing. I knew God. I rejoiced in God my Saviour.'[131] Once she had recovered enough to ride, she went to rest and recuperate at Sheep-Hill, a tiny place near the village of Burnopfield, which was about ten miles away. After making a surprisingly quick recovery she returned to Newcastle and resumed her work with the classes and bands and her visits to the sick and backsliders:

'My labour was now again my delight. My soul was stayed upon God continually. I had no doubt of his love. I had no fear of his wrath, and no desire but to do and suffer his will.... [I was] wholly athirst for God, the living God.'[132]

Wesley's visit to Newcastle had proved very successful with so many flocking to hear him at the Orphan House that it could not contain them all, but the need for him elsewhere led to his departure at the end of April. When he returned to Newcastle on 18 September 1745 the city was in an uproar because news had just arrived that Bonnie Prince Charlie's forces had seized Edinburgh and, in his words, 'fear and darkness were now on every side.'[133] This was made worse when news of the British army's defeat at Prestonpans reached the city on 21 September. Wesley instantly wrote a letter of patriotic support to the Mayor:

130 JWLL pg 52
131 ibid
132 JWLL pg 52-3
133 JWJ 19 Nov 1745

'All I can do for His Majesty, whom I honour and love – I think not less than I did my own father – is this: I cry unto God day by day, in public and in private, to put all his enemies to confusion. And I exhort all that hear me to do the same, and in their several stations, to exert themselves as loyal subjects, who so long as they fear God cannot but honour the King.'[134]

Some of the city's inhabitants fled while others helped mount the cannon on the city walls. Wesley attended worship at St Andrew's, the church in which Grace had grown up. He records that its vicar, John Ellison, preached 'strong and weighty' though he could 'scarce conclude for tears'.[135] It is clear from Wesley's writings that he attributed the military success of the Jacobites to God. It was God's punishment for the 'senseless wickedness, the ignorant profaneness… and the wanton blasphemy' of the troops loyal to the King.[136]

Wesley left Newcastle on 4 November. In December he wrote to Grace asking her to take on the role of housekeeper from Mrs Jackson at the Orphan House. At first she was averse to doing that but then she felt that God was calling her to take on the responsibility. On Christmas Eve she left her base at Sheep-Hill and on Christmas Day took up her new post. It marked a significant increase in her workload because there were always a range of activities taking place within the Orphan House and that meant there were always visitors to look after. No precise description of the housekeeper's role has survived, but we know that it was not just confined to managing the cleaning, catering, and so on, because Wesley told Sarah Perrin, who was the equivalent housekeeper at the New Room in Bristol, that her role was to make sure it was a house of faith and that she

134 JWJ 21 Sept 1745
135 JWJ 22 Nov 1745
136 Letter to Mayor 26 Oct 1745 Northumberland Record Office

should tackle any society member who was not showing 'the fruits of faith, either of holiness or good works'. Sarah also had to organise the sale of Methodist hymnbooks and other publications from the New Room.

When John Wesley arrived back in Newcastle on 26 February 1746 he discovered Grace was in a state of complete exhaustion from all that was being demanded of her. This was not surprising because for three weeks she had also been directly responsible for nursing two sick men: a weaver called John Haughton, who was one of the trustees of the Orphan House, and a travelling preacher from Cornwall called William Shepherd. She had scarce had time to sleep properly and, as a consequence, was suffering from fainting fits. Understandably some society members protested on Grace's behalf and John decided that he had been amiss in not providing her with a helper. He therefore ordered her to rest and appointed a woman called Mary Proctor as her assistant. This enabled Grace from then on to split her week. She would spend Saturday to Tuesday undertaking her duties at the Orphan House and Wednesday to Friday in accommodation in Sheep-hill, travelling around the surrounding villages, visiting bands, classes, and the sick and dealing with anyone judged to be a backslider. Increasingly the male preachers, both those who were local and those who were visiting itinerants, came to respect her for what she was achieving.

Wesley left Newcastle again on 17 March 1746. By then he had introduced Grace to the lay preacher John Bennet for the first time – it was an encounter that was to change the lives of all three of them.

John Wesley travelling with one of his lay preachers (from print in 'Wesley His Own Biographer' published 1891)

3

Her Two Suitors

The thirty-two year old lay preacher John Bennet was the son of William Bennet, a prosperous yeoman farmer from Whitehaugh, near the village of what is now called Chinley but which was then known as Four Lanes End in Derbyshire. Its main feature was a large nonconformist chapel, which had been built in 1711, and its minister, Dr James Clegg, was a major influence on the family. Bennet was educated at a school in the nearby market town of Chapel-en-le-Frith and his father intended his son to become an attorney. John instead preferred to begin training as a minister and for a time he attended Findern Academy near Derby. However, in 1732 he turned his back on religion and, in his words, 'let go the reins of passion', taking 'infinitely more pleasure in vice than virtue'.[137] He became first a magistrate's clerk in Sheffield and then a 'jagger' or carrier of lead ore, salt, and other goods. This gave him an excellent knowledge of an area that stretched from Sheffield to Macclesfield. It was while Bennet was engaged in that work that he was attracted back to Christianity in 1741 by hearing the preaching of David Taylor, an itinerant freelance evangelist, on Sheffield Moor. He subsequently had what he describes as 'a miraculous vision' and from then on he devoted himself to serving God:

'Filled with wonder and delight… from that moment I found a

137 JBD pg15

disinclination and abhorrence of all sin, and was sensible of that horrible ingratitude I had all my life shown to the God of my life, and to that blessed Redeemer'.[138]

Through Taylor, John Bennet was introduced to the Rev. Benjamin Ingham, the Yorkshire-born friend of Charles Wesley and the man who had accompanied the Wesleys in their work in America. Bennet found Ingham to be a truly inspirational preacher and he accompanied him ever further afield into Yorkshire, Lancashire and Cheshire. He first heard John Wesley preach in May 1742 and he agreed to link himself to the Methodists the following April, largely through the influence of the lay preacher John Nelson, a stonemason from Birstall. As Bennet noted in his journal, Methodist 'was not a name which we took upon ourselves but one fixed upon us by way of reproach without our approbation or consent'.[139] That summer Bennet worked alongside Charles Wesley and the two men became friends. Within a year he had not only taken over responsibility for guiding the Methodist societies around Bradford and Leeds in Yorkshire but also become the leading figure in developing new societies in Cheshire and Derbyshire. This was against the wishes of his father, who threatened to disinherit him. Only his mother was prepared to support what he was doing.

The importance of 'Mr Bennet's Circuit' can be inferred by the fact that he was one of only four lay preachers to be invited to the first ever Wesleyan Methodist Conference in 1744. It was this Conference that established what was expected of lay preachers (or 'helpers' or 'assistants' as John Wesley preferred to call them). It was agreed that they would be used only where there was no ordained minister to voice the gospel and that, wherever possible, they would

138 JBD pg 22-23
139 JBD pg 25

use private homes rather than preach in the open air so as to reduce the danger of attack from the mob. It was acceptable for them to receive food and clothing but they were to take no money for their work and, in addition to preaching, their role was to regularly meet up with the bands and classes 'to feed and guide, to teach and govern the flock' and so ensure society members lived up to the demands of their faith.[140] The Conference also defined the roles of society stewards, class-leaders, and others. It has been stated that Bennet's participation in this Conference made him effectively one of the architects of early Methodist connexionalism. He also attended the next Methodist Conference in 1745. Its main focus was on ensuring that what was preached was theologically sound and that the societies were properly organised.

Bennet arrived in Newcastle on 27 February 1746, the day after John Wesley, and Grace's first impression of him was simply of 'a gentleman in black'.[141] She says that he was immediately taken very ill and that Wesley asked her to nurse him. This was what she was to do for the next six months and during that time she says that her heart was 'drawn out to pray with and for him'.[142] She and Bennet were, of course, of similar age because he was just two years older than her. Despite her best endeavours and those of a doctor it looked at first as if he was going to die. Grace sent for his family to come and see him because she was so sure his death was imminent. Nevertheless, she still pleaded with God that Bennet should recover and, to everyone's amazement, the sick man suddenly cried out that all his pain had gone and that he felt well again. From then on he slowly but surely began to recover. Both she and Bennet saw this as a personal answer to her prayers. It was almost inevitable that Bennet fell in love with her and, when he voiced that, he gave Grace the

140 See Minutes of 1744 Conference
141 GBM pg 18. Grace gives the date erroneously as 27 April.
142 ibid

impression that this was destined. She was to repeatedly say: 'God gave ME to him for a wife'.[143]

However, there was no talk between them of any immediate wedding. That is not surprising. Bennet was well aware that his lifestyle as an itinerant preacher did not suit marriage. He was hardly ever at home. It was also the case that John Wesley had made quite clear that he opposed his preachers marrying because he thought this distracted them from giving everything to serving God:

'[If you marry] are you seeking to supply the want of… intercourse with God by the enjoyment of a creature? You imagine that near connexion with a woman will make amends for distance from God!… Has your experience taught you no better than this? You were happy once… in God without being beholden to any creature… [Are you] not loving the creature more than the Creator? Does it not imply that you are a lover of pleasure more than a lover of God?'[144]

We know from Bennet's journal that, prior to meeting Grace, he had deliberately suppressed his feelings for other women. He thought the Devil was trying to snare him away from his preaching by tempting him with young women. For example, he recounts the following dream that he had about a young girl called Mary Brocklehurst:

'I dreamed I was invited to a house… and there was present Mary Brocklehurst, her mother, sister and brother William. They invited me to their house. I went to bed and thought I heard some person breathe towards my feet. So I felt my foot touch another and found great love, so reaching my hand down

143 GBM pg 19
144 Thoughts upon Marriage in JW Works (1872 edition) Vol XI pg 464-465

I felt a hand in mine, it was Mary Brocklehurst's. She lay with a young woman, a relation, so they both got up and came to my bedside. I told them if I had known it had been them we would have lain together. She said that would not be right. I told her I had such value for her soul I doubted not doing that without lust. She felt the same.'[145]

In the light of this historians have usually suggested that it was entirely Bennet's decision to avoid any formal declaration of marriage at this stage, but it is possible that it was a mutual decision. Grace was also a preacher, even if she lacked the official authorisation that was being given to men. It was natural for both of them to think that it was better to leave any discussion of marriage to a later stage. In the interval they promised to engage in regular correspondence with each other. Such an approach was certainly not unusual – recent research has shown that just over half of Wesley's bachelor preachers got married and most of them did so only as their itinerant work was ceasing.

Shortly after Bennet had left, Grace acquired another lay preacher as her patient. This was Thomas Westell, who had arrived to preach in the Newcastle area in the summer. A cabinet maker from Bristol, he had been one of the very first lay preachers appointed by the Wesleys.[146] Newcastle was rife with disease because of the overcrowded housing and lack of any proper sanitation and Westell was taken ill with a fever. No sooner had he begun to recover then Grace fell ill herself and she was in bed for three weeks. Her response was to tell her assistant Sarah Proctor: 'God has laid me upon this bed that I may have time for prayer.'[147] Grace and Westell clearly

---

145 12 Sept 1742 JBD pg 59

146 The first five had been called 'the sons of the gospel': they were John Cennick, Thomas Maxfield, Joseph Humphreys, Thomas Richards, and Thomas Westell.

147 JWLL pg 54

became friends. There is no hint in that of anything sexual. What Grace writes about is how spiritually uplifting it was to be constantly alongside the preacher. For example, she provides an account of how one night she and Westell went up onto the roof of the Orphan House and talked about how God was closer to them than the Devil and how they then went back down to the kitchen and sang hymns together till it was past midnight. She and Westell then spent a week scarce doing anything but praying all day and night, sometimes till two o'clock in the morning.

It is easy to see how such behaviour led to gossip about Grace's behaviour, even if, from her perspective, the outcome was her spiritual improvement. One of the noticeable differences in the evidence that has survived on Grace as opposed to some of the other female leaders is the lack of any correspondence between her and other women. This may be just an historical accident or it may indicate that Grace was much more comfortable working alongside men. That – and her total abhorrence of gossiping – may help explain why she did not endear herself to some women, especially those who were jealous of her closeness to John Wesley. Sarah Perrin, the housekeeper at the New Room, faced similar hostility from some of the female society members in Bristol. Sarah found it very difficult that much of what she did had 'a false construction' placed upon it and that 'the more I desire the good of all, the less I am beloved'.[148] She told John how some of the women had told her to distance herself from him:

'I have had a caution given me not to write so freely because my affection has been misinterpreted; lest it should hurt the cause of God. But I cannot see, if we feel love and thankfulness for the blessings we receive from your ministry, why we should

148 31 May 1744. Wesley had this letter published in the Arminian Magazine in March 1778 pg 222

refrain from speaking about it, whilst the world are so ready to open their mouths against you. That we shall always find more nearness to some souls than others, I am firmly persuaded... Therefore I think, as my soul prospers, the same love I have always expressed, will increase... My heart is knit more and more to you.'[149]

Towards the end of their time together Grace says she and Thomas Westell fasted until 'our souls were filled as with marrow and fatness'.[150] Westell then led the worship at a meeting of the bands and the result was a real sense of God's presence:

'I was constrained to break out into loud prayer. A cry went forth. Many wept. Many praised God. All (but four) were filled with consolation.'[151]

She adds that over the next few days there was a real sense of revival in the Orphan House, which was 'filled in an unusual manner with peace and joy in the Holy Ghost'.[152] It was during this time that Grace's mother came to believe that she was assured of salvation. and that, on 23 October, Charles Wesley arrived in Newcastle with Edward Perronet as his travelling companion.[153] Edward was the son of the Wesleys' close friend, Vincent Perronet, the Vicar of Shoreham. He was a highly educated young man, having studied at St John's College in Cambridge. Three days later Perronet went

---

149 10 June 1744. ibid pg 223

150 JWLL pg 55

151 ibid

152 JWLL pg 56

153 Grace says that she cried out at breakfast: 'I see Mr Charles Wesley. He is not far off' a few minutes before he actually entered the city gates (JWLL pg 71). Augustin Leger points out that this apparent clairvoyance was not what it seems: the men would have been expected and their probable time of arrival known.

down with a fever and Grace began nursing him. Charles Wesley saw the young man's recovery as an answer to prayer:

'We prayed for him in strong faith, nothing doubting. Monday and Tuesday he grew worse and worse. On Wednesday the smallpox appeared – a favourable sort. Yet on Thursday we were much alarmed by the great pain and danger he was in. We had recourse to our never failing remedy, and received a most remarkable, immediate answer to our prayer. The great means of his recovery was the prayer of faith.'[154]

Charles Wesley preached across the Newcastle area until the end of December and then set off south with Perronet. Shortly afterwards Thomas Westell announced he was also leaving. Grace and an itinerant lay preacher called Robert Swindells, who was on his way to Cheshire, agreed to accompany him for the first day of his journey south. It was said of Swindells that he was 'never known to say an unkind word of anyone' and he had a reputation for being exceptionally caring to the poor:

'He not only gave them all the money he could spare himself but sometimes gave part of his own raiment, which he at times could ill spare, and also frequently begged money and clothes of others to supply their wants.'[155]

All three stopped at Ferryhill, a small town on the medieval Great North Road, and there Grace and Robert Swindells threw lots to determine which of them would continue to travel with Westell

---

154 CWJ 26 Oct 1746
155 C. Atmore, The Methodist Memorial, Bristol 1801 pg 409

into Yorkshire.[156] The outcome was a decision in favour of Grace. According to her she had had a premonition that this would happen and so she had taken with her a spare gown and some linen. This makes it sound as if the action was premeditated. It certainly marked another step up in Grace's developing role. There were two types of lay preacher – those who used the little spare time they had when they were not working to preach locally and those who had given up their employment in order to become full-time itinerant preachers, travelling around the country at John Wesley's direction. Grace's preaching role had essentially been confined to the area around Newcastle and it had been undertaken at times that fitted in around her duties at the Orphan House. Now she was committing herself to travelling more widely, even though she could not afford to relinquish her role as housekeeper because, as a woman, she was not eligible to have the status and funding of being an itinerant preacher.

It has been suggested that Grace took this significant step because she wanted to go south so she could meet Bennet again, but she does not say that. What comes across in her account is her desire to engage in the work of God and how exciting and enjoyable she found that to be. On the journey south she spoke to the women while Westell addressed the men, although there were also occasions when she spoke to mixed groups. She found the experience to be a very positive one: 'I found it was good to be among them: and God gave us many blessings together.'[157] However, she knew she could only be away from the Orphan House for a limited time. She got as far south as Lincolnshire and then returned to Newcastle in February 1747. Not surprisingly, she faced a very hostile reception for having gone off with Westell. Everyone accepted that itinerant preachers should

---

156 This was a practice that the Methodists had copied from the Moravians. The Wesleys had observed Moravian missionaries using lots in America. It was the method used by John Wesley in deciding whether or not to go to Bristol in 1739 – the step that directly led to him undertaking open-air preaching.

157 JWLL pg 57

never travel alone because of the dangers they faced, but it was not expected that they would choose a female companion. It confirmed in a number of minds that Grace was having an affair with Westell.

On 2 March John Wesley arrived and he spent some days every week examining the religious societies round Newcastle. He says he found 'great cause to rejoice over them'.[158] The travelling he engaged in was quite extensive, covering places like Gateshead, Blanchland, Newlands, Sunderland, South Biddick, Hexham, and Horsley. Wesley makes no reference to Grace's presence in his published journal but we know she accompanied him, just as she had accompanied Westell. More significantly, when Wesley headed south, she opted to travel with him for a time , probably getting as far as Osmotherley in North Yorkshire, where he met up with the lay preacher John Nelson. This was not a wise move on her part because it caused the gossiping tongues in Newcastle to wag even more.

Whatever Grace's failings, she did not lack either courage or commitment. If she felt she was doing what God wanted, no amount of criticism deterred her. She therefore ignored the tittle-tattle on her return and accepted the invitation of Christopher Hopper to accompany him on a preaching tour of Allendale in the south west of Northumberland. Hopper was the twenty-five year old son of a farmer from Ryton in County Durham and the teacher in the school at Sheep-hill. He had joined the Methodists in 1743 and commenced preaching shortly afterwards. He was a happily married man and there is no hint of anything sexual in him seeking Grace's company. He simply respected her abilities. She provides a vivid account of the role she played:

'We met every night [for prayers]....[and] in the daytime partly

---

158 JWJ 19 March 1747. He says that the number of members had fallen to around four hundred at the Orphan House but those who remained 'breathed nothing but love and brotherly kindness'.

the people came to me and partly I went to them. By this means I spoke with all the members (as well as many others) and divided the believers into bands. I had at first designed to stay only a week, but the work of God so mightily prevailed and the poor people were so importunate with me that I could not break away till I had spent a month with them.'[159]

All during this time Grace had been in occasional correspondence with John Bennet and in June 1747 she decided to go to London where the annual conference was being held. She almost certainly hoped to see him there. If she thought their reunion might speed up the possibility of them getting married, she was disappointed. Bennet was still totally committed to his work. One of the topics under discussion at the conference was the immense geographical size of the Yorkshire circuit. It was agreed that it should be split so that Cheshire would have its own circuit. This would also cover Lancashire and Derbyshire and the cities of Sheffield and Nottingham. Effectively this recognised the importance of 'Mr Bennet's Circuit'. Over the next couple of years Bennet was to develop a regular travelling pattern that was hugely demanding. He would leave his home in Chinley and follow a route that took him through various Derbyshire villages to Taddington. Next he would travel through various Cheshire villages before heading north to Manchester, Shakerley, Bolton, and the Rossendale area of Lancashire. Sometimes he would go further north as far as Kirkby Lonsdale and Kendal in Cumbria. He would also usually at some stage go to Haworth so he could assist Rev. William Grimshaw, then the main clerical supporter of the Wesleys, in the 'Great Haworth Round'. This involved visiting various villages and towns in Yorkshire, including Halifax, Bradford and Leeds.

159 JWLL pg 57-8

After the Conference John Wesley spent part of August travelling around the societies in Yorkshire, Lancàshire and Cheshire that relied heavily on Nelson, Bennet, and the Scottish shoemaker and peddler, William Darnay, a preacher who as yet had not linked himself with the Wesleys.[160] That autumn John Wesley signalled out Bennet and Nelson as two of the preachers with whom he was most pleased, saying they were 'cordially united in carrying on the Lord's work'.[161] During all this time Grace was back at the Orphan House. She acted as nurse to two preachers, Eleazor Webster and Edward Dunstable, in July and August and then to a third, James Wheatley, from September. Wheatley became particularly enamoured with her and Grace says 'he would suffer none but me to come to him'.[162] In his case she may have been a bit naïve because Wheatley was a known womaniser, whom Charles Wesley was later to try and expel because of his adulterous behaviour with seven women in the Bristol circuit. It may have been Wheatley's behaviour that contributed to tongues waxing ever more maliciously against Grace:

'Some of our sisters began to... make many objections to me. I did all I could to remove them. I called frequently upon them, and spoke as lovingly as I could. But it did not avail. They were still equally displeased and endeavoured to spread the same spirit among others. But I did not as yet perceive any resentment towards them: only I was grieved, because they hurt their souls.' [163]

The attitude of other women stands in sharp contrast to the high

---

160 Darnay eventually joined Wesley in 1747.

161 Letter to Grimshaw 27 Nov 1747 quoted in J.W. Laycock, Methodist Heroes in the Great Haworth Round 1734-84, Wadsworth & Co, Keighley 1909 pg 57

162 JWLL pg 58

163 JWS pg 58-59

regard in which some of the men held Grace. When the Rev. William Stamp wrote the first major history of the Orphan House in 1863 he concluded that Grace had been 'an instrument of great good' because she combined piety with 'skilful and efficient management', an 'affectionate and winning' manner, and 'a ready utterance'. It was his assessment that she 'rendered the Orphan House 'a hallowed and favourite home' for all the preachers who temporarily visited it. [164] Although written with Victorian hyperbole, his conclusion is sound. The very fact so many preachers wanted her to accompany them shows how much they admired her qualities. One modern historian has described her as 'the pick of the pack' in Newcastle.[165]

Neither John nor Charles Wesley visited Newcastle in the autumn or winter of 1747 or the first half of 1748 because of commitments elsewhere. John, for example, spent most of his time in London, in the south-west and in Ireland. By this stage there was growing unrest among the bachelor lay preachers at Wesley's insistence they should remain single. This is not surprising. A small but significant minority of the lay preachers had been married before they took up their itinerant work and their married status did not seem to weaken their service to God. Indeed some, like John Nelson, were among the most effective. Moreover, four of the key clerical supporters of the revival were married – George Whitefield, Benjamin Ingham, William Grimshaw, and Vincent Perronet. The topic of marriage therefore became a major item of discussion at the 1748 Methodist Conference. John Wesley did not veto that because he was beginning to have doubts about whether his personal vow to remain celibate was necessary. Further study of the early Church had begun to make him realise that it had not been as opposed to marriage as he had originally thought and he had started to think

---

164 W. Stamp, The Orphan House of Wesley, J. Mason 1863 pg 48
165 T. Crichton Mitchell, Charles Wesley: Man with the Dancing Heart, Beacon Hill Press 1994 pg 102

of all those whom he had met who claimed a wife improved their ability to serve God.[166]

That there might be a woman who could help him serve God more effectively had once seemed to him impossible. He had always said he would never be able to find a wife equal to his mother. However, he now felt that he had met 'a very few women' who matched Susanna 'in knowledge and piety'. Some of these women were sufficiently wealthy that they could easily more than financially replace the income he received from his fellowship at Oxford (money that he would lose if he married). There was no danger that they would require resources that would better be spent on serving the poor. None of the women he had in mind would expect him to provide them with a comfortable lifetsyle. What he heard at the Conference did not make John publicly declare a change of policy but the voices in favour of permitting marriage were sufficiently eloquent to make him concede that 'a believer might marry without suffering loss in the soul'.[167] He was later to write that the Catholic Church had done a great disservice to Christianity by first encouraging and then demanding celibacy for priests:

'The Apostle [Paul] on the contrary says, Marriage is honourable in all' (Heb. Xiii 4) and accuses those who 'forbid to marry' of teaching 'doctrines of devils'. How lawful it was for the clergy to marry, his directions show (1 Tim.iv 1,3). And how convenient, yea necessary, in many cases it is, clearly appears from the innumerable mischiefs which have in all ages followed the prohibition of it in the Church of Rome.'[168]

---

166 He mentions in particular a physician in Rotterdam called Dr Koker whom he had met in 1738 whilst visiting the Moravians: 'He often declared he was never so much free from care, never served God with so little distraction, as since his marriage with one, who was both able and willing to bear that care for him'.

167 JWLL pg 1

168 Popery Calmly Considered in Works (1872 edition) Vol X pg 154-5

The Conference debate must have been of equal interest to John Bennet, given his promise of eventual marriage to Grace, but it was also of particular concern to Charles Wesley because in April 1748 he had secretly proposed to Sarah Gwynne, the young daughter of a Welsh landowner and magistrate sympathetic to Methodism. For Charles and her it was a question of love at first sight. However, Sally (as she was known) was nineteen years younger than Charles and her age and aristocratic background hardly suited her for assisting in the work of the religious revival. For that reason Charles had not yet said anything about this to his brother, even though he had promised never to offer marriage to anyone without first seeking his approval. Indeed it was only in June that Charles had summoned the courage to secretly ask Sally's parents whether they would give their approval. At the time of the Conference the Gwynnes had not yet given this, largely because of their understandable concern that Sally did not know what she was letting herself in for and that Charles lacked the income to support a family.

After the Conference John headed north and he arrived in Newcastle on 9 July. He was delighted to find that numbers there had increased. In addition to visiting and examining societies across the region over the next few weeks, he went on a preaching tour that took him as far north as Berwick. In his published journal he makes a passing reference to being taken ill. He says that on 1 August he began suffering from a headache and that he tried to ignore it, but it got progressively worse until by the 6 August he was also having bouts of sickness. He cured this by taking a dose of ipecacuanha, which was a medicine used to stop vomiting. This journal account hides a far more significant event. Grace Murray says Wesley was sufficiently ill that week that she had to 'be with him much, both day and night' and that, as a consequence, 'he spoke to me more freely than before'.[169]

What she meant by this is clarified by John's account of his sickness that was not written for publication:

'I was taken ill at Newcastle. Grace Murray attended me continually. I observed her more narrowly than ever before, both as to her temper, sense, and behaviour. I esteemed and loved her more and more. And, when I was a little recovered, I told her, sliding into it I know not how, 'If ever I marry, I think you will be that person'. After some time I spoke to her more directly. She seemed utterly amazed and said, 'This is too great a blessing for me: I can't tell how to believe it. This is all I could have wished for under Heaven, if I had dared wish for it.' From that time I conversed with her as my own.' [170]

He also subsequently embodied the moment of her acceptance in verse:

'Abash'd she spake, 'O what is this,
Far above all my boldest hope!
Can God, beyond my utmost wish,
Thus lift his worthless handmaid up?
This only could my soul desire:
This only (had I dar'd) require.'[171]

When he applied his charm John could turn the head of most single women and Grace would have been hugely flattered by having a man of his standing propose to her. Not surprisingly a number of historians have suggested that her positive response was more that

169 JWLL pg 59
170 JWLL pg 1-2
171 JW's Poem on Grace Murray

of a worshipper than a prospective bride:

'To Grace Murray Wesley's offer must have seemed like the command of King Ahasuerus to Esther to share his throne. He was not only her superior in education and social standing, he was her spiritual guide and the revered and autocratic head of the whole community of which she formed part.'[172]

Simon Ross Valentine, the biographer of John Bennet, shares that view:

'How could a woman such as Grace Murray stand before Wesley and disagree with him? How could she reject an offer of marriage given by man who claimed divine approbation for the proposal, even though she loved another? How could a former servant, with little education and influence, disagree with a man who, by charisma and the emotive power of his stentorian voice, could cause crowds of thousands to fall silent and listen to his every word?'[173]

Other historians have gone further and stated she was motivated by a desire for fame and eminence – although attributing such a motive replies entirely on accepting the gossip of her enemies.

There is no doubt that John Wesley's words were unexpected. She had known him for eight years and in all that time he had expressed nothing of this kind. Moreover, it was common knowledge that he had committed himself to never marrying. Grace says his proposal surprised her 'as if the moon had dropped out of her orbit' and that part of her could not believe that she was hearing aright because 'it

---

172 D.M. Jones, Charles Wesley: A Study, Skeffington & Son Ltd pg 163
173 John Bennet and the Origins of the Evangelical Revival in England, Scarecrow Press 1997 pg 228

seemed too strange to be true.'[174] In his account John implies that Grace had been in love with him virtually ever since they had met and, had he spoken earlier, she would never have made any kind of implied commitment to Bennet. Of her suitability as a wife Wesley wrote:

'I saw her run, with winged speed
In works of faith and labouring love:
I saw her glorious toil succeed,
And showers of blessings from above
Crowning her warm effectual prayer,
And glorified my God in her.'[175]

It is easy to see what John saw in her. Grace was attractive and still relatively young, she had shown a deep commitment to the work of the revival for a number of years, and she had shown her loving nature in nursing him. Writing in 1910, the historian Augustin Leger suggested that John was attracted to Grace because he knew she was a woman he could easily dominate and control. That may also be true. John knew it was important for the work of the revival that, should he marry, his wife should not oppose his continued itinerancy.

In the heat of the moment Grace's initial response was to say nothing to Wesley about the understanding that she and Bennet had about one day getting married. There is no doubt that she really liked Bennet, but did she truly love him? Absence does not necessarily make the heart grow fonder and she had not really had any quality time with the lay preacher for eighteen months. Moreover, Bennet had shown as yet no sign that he would ever marry her. Only in

174 JWLL pg 59
175 JW's Poem on Grace Murray

the coming weeks and months did this prior commitment begin to weigh heavily with Grace's conscience. Then she increasingly began to wish that Wesley had spoken of his love before she had made any kind of prior promise to Bennet. It is not clear exactly when Grace first spoke to Wesley about this but, given what happened shortly afterwards, it is reasonable to assume she said nothing about her relationship with Bennet until much later. That was to prove a mistake.

John's proposal came with only one caveat. He told Grace that she must not tell anyone until he had first discussed his desire to marry her with Charles Wesley. He informed her how he and his brother had promised that they would never marry without consulting with each other first. John, of course, did not yet know that Charles had already broken his part of this agreement. To this caveat Grace readily acceded. Wesley was committed to leaving Newcastle on 16 August and he provides us with the following account of the conversation he had with Grace on the night before he left:

> 'I told her, 'I am convinced God has called you to be my fellow-labourer in the gospel. I will trust we shall part no more.' She begged me might not part so soon, saying, 'It was more than she could bear.'[176]

The outcome of this exchange was that Grace accompanied him on a preaching itinerary that took them to County Durham, Yorkshire, Derbyshire, and Lancashire. It is, of course, possible that Grace hoped this would give her the opportunity to see Bennet and extricate herself from her promise to him before speaking of their relationship to Wesley. It is also true that travelling together gave John more time to judge whether his proposal made sense. He was a

176 JWLL pg 2

man who liked to justify his actions in his own mind. Even as a child his father had said of him: 'He will have a reason for everything he has to do. I suppose he will not even break wind unless he had a reason for it.'[177]

Wesley preached at Stockton, Yarm and Osmotherley en route to Leeds, which they reached on 17 August. Over the next few days he preached there and in Wakefield, Bradford and other neighbouring towns. On 24 August Wesley and Grace arrived at Haworth where the Rev. William Grimshaw welcomed them. He fully updated Wesley on the violence which the Methodists were facing in that area. Wesley refused to be intimidated and the three of them moved on to the Lancashire village of Roughlee, where two preachers, Thomas Colbeck, a grocer from Keighley, and William Mackford, a grain trader from Newcastle, joined them. Grace knew Colbeck very well because he was a trustee of the Orphan House. Wesley decided to preach in the shadow of Pendle Hill and a mob of around five hundred men stormed down on him and the others. It must have been a very frightening experience for Grace. Many of the men had been drinking and were armed with clubs and staves. Their leader demanded that Wesley should go with him so he could be taken before the authorities at Barrowford. Wesley agreed but that did not prevent one of the mob punching him in the face and another throwing a stick at him.

Seeing the danger they were in, Grimshaw urged Grace to seek safety by immediately returning to the village of Roughlee. He promised he and the others would do what they could to protect John from further attack. She did as she was bid and, once she was back in Roughlee, began leading a prayer meeting, petitioning God that John and the others would be permitted to return safely. John's companions found it no easy task to protect him on the journey to

177 Cited in S. Tomkins, John Wesley: A Biography, Lion 2003 pg 15

Barrowford. Grimshaw was subjected to a severe manhandling and lost his wig. Colbeck was thrown to the ground and badly kicked. Mackford was rolled in the mud until it was thought he had been killed. Grace was left not knowing what had happened for a couple of hours. Only then did John and the others return, having been released from the mob by the orders of the magistrate. Poor William Mackford was to retain permanent injuries from the beating that he had received.

In the aftermath of this debacle the party moved on and met up with John Bennet at Milner's Barn on 27 August. The presence of Grace must have come as a huge surprise to him. What he was yet to find out was that she was now hopelessly entangled in a relationship with his leader.

John Bennet (John Rylands Library)

4

GRACE'S PROMISE TO MARRY JOHN BENNET

For four days John Wesley, John Bennet and Grace Murray travelled together through a bleak landscape. The countryside had been devastated by severe floods, which had hit the area the previous month. The journals of both John Wesley and John Bennet record the violence that happened when the two men attempted to preach at Bolton on 28 August 1748, but Wesley's version is the more vivid of the two:

> 'As soon as I began speaking they began thrusting to and fro, endeavouring to throw me down from the steps on which I stood. They did so once or twice; but I went up again and continued my discourse. Then they began to throw stones; at the same time some got upon the Cross behind me to push me down... One man was bawling just at my ear when a stone struck him on the cheek, and he was still. A second was forcing his way down to me, till another stone hit him on the forehead.... The third, being close to me, stretched out his hand, and in an instant a sharp stone came upon the joints of his fingers'.[178]

Fortunately a local officer halted the mob before any further harm could happen. Afterwards they visited Shackerley, Davyhulme,

178 JWJ 28 August 1748

Oldfield Brow, and Stockport before arriving at Bennet's home in Chinley on 31 August.

During those four days neither Wesley nor Bennet appear to have given any inkling to each other of their feelings for Grace. The fact that Wesley decided Grace should stay under Bennet's protection at Chinley whilst he headed back to deal with issues in London, almost certainly indicates that as yet Grace had not told him about her prior attachment to the lay preacher. Historians have tended to assume that Bennet was still as attached to Grace as he had been when he intimated he wanted to marry her. However, that may not have been the case. He had had no physical contact with her and we know that in July 1748 he had been working alongside a female preacher called Grace Walton. Unfortunately we know nothing much about her or whether there was any intimacy between them.[179] Interestingly Bennet's journal is very circumspect about what happened between him and Grace once Wesley had left. He says nothing about her presence until 7 September, when he describes taking her to Buxton and then Taddington, and adds: 'We spoke our minds freely together touching some things that had long lain on my mind.'[180] According to what Grace later told Wesley, Bennet formally asked her to marry him. Given it took him so long to propose, one must wonder whether it took that time for his love for her to be rekindled. His proposal certainly then threw her into a quandary. She knew Bennet was expecting her to honour the understanding they had possessed and yet she could not explain her new situation because she had promised Wesley she would keep

179 The entry in Bennet's journal for 10 July says: 'Grace Walton exhorted at five and afterwards we went together towards Milner's Barn. I exhorted at Milner's Barn in the evening.' The entry on 11 July says: 'We went to the Quarterly Meeting at Woodley'. JBD pg 191. A 1761 letter from JW to Grace Walton has survived but its focus is largely on encouraging her to examine her faith more. There is also a reference to Grace Walton in a letter from John Wesley written in 1769 but it merely states how in the past he had given her advice on how she should 'intermix short exhortations with prayer' rather than speak 'in a continued discourse', which would be judged preaching. Works (1872 edition) Vol XII pg 355
180 JBD pg 174

their relationship a secret.

Because she was uncertain how to handle the situation, Grace made no immediate response, but this only made matters worse. Bennet kept asking for an answer. She eventually came up with what she thought was a way out of her dilemma. She said she would marry Bennet but only if John Wesley gave his consent. Some historians have suggested this shows she was a flirt who enjoyed having the attentions of two men. However, this view has little to commend it. Neither Wesley nor Bennet ever interpreted her actions in that way. Far from enjoying the attentions of the two men, Grace is consistently presented in Wesley's account as being deeply unhappy about her invidious position. Some historians have implied Grace would not have given a qualified 'yes' unless she was more in love with Bennet than with Wesley, but that is not borne out by some of her later actions. For that reason others have suggested she was just too weak-willed to give a direct 'no' to a forceful Bennet. It is true that Grace, despite possessing courage and determination as a preacher, was weak when it came to standing up to Wesley or Bennet because of the respect in which she held them.

Nevertheless, the best explanation for her action comes from Wesley himself. He gives two reasons. The first was that, after considering the matter, Grace concluded she had no alternative but to say 'yes' because the lay preacher had the prior claim on her hand: 'She believed it was the will of God'.[181] The second was that she did not want to hurt Bennet's feelings and feared what would happen if she declined him. Grace was still very unhappy about what had happened to John Brydon after she had rejected him as a suitor and she had no desire to have a similar impact on Bennet and so be responsible for the revival losing his talents. If we accept Wesley's judgement, then it seems not unreasonable to surmise that Grace

181 JWLL pg 2

felt she was doing the honourable thing in saying she would marry Bennet whilst simultaneously giving Wesley the means of preventing that. She presumably felt that Wesley would more ably handle the situation and that he would persuade Bennet to relinquish his claim on her without that causing any breakdown in relationships or any harm to the revival.

Wesley says that Grace's acceptance left her in 'deep distress' because she wanted to marry him and not Bennet. He also says (and this is presumably based on what Grace later told him) that Bennet was understandably puzzled by his prospective bride's obvious unhappiness. He therefore sought to reassure Grace that his love for her was no less than on the day he first expressed his wish to marry her. He may well have assumed that she was annoyed that it had taken him so long to properly formalise their relationship. It was only when she refused to embrace him and pushed him away that Bennet became suspicious that she might have feelings for someone else. That night he dreamt that he saw John Wesley voicing his passion for Grace. In the morning he told her about this and directly asked her whether there was anything going on between them. She replied that there was not. In his account Wesley says it was a mistake for her to lie but this was done 'partly out of love and partly out of fear of exposing me'.[182]

Without questioning her further Bennet took Grace to see his sister and he spent a little time showing her the beautiful scenery around his home. Grace then went with him on a preaching tour to Sheffield and Leeds. He told Grace they would get married as soon as they had Wesley's permission and it was mutually agreed that both of them would write requesting this. One can imagine the shock that Wesley experienced when he opened their letters. We do not know what Bennet wrote but Wesley says that Grace's letter

---

182 JWLL pg 3 John Wesley says that the story of the dream was told to him by Bennet.

stated that her acceptance was based on the assumption it was God's will that she should marry Bennet because of her prior agreement with him. This to Wesley appeared a total nonsense because he had already come to the conclusion that God had been preparing Grace to become his 'fellow labourer' for ten years by what he was later to call 'a wonderful train of providences.'[183]

The couple appear to have agreed to go back to their respective duties until they received Wesley's response. On 14 September Bennet resumed his normal round of preaching engagements and Grace returned north to her duties in Newcastle. It was at this time that Bennet made his biggest contribution to the future organisation of Methodism. Back in July he had been contemplating how to better link together the religious societies he was visiting. His solution was to suggest that the leaders of the various classes within the societies should meet together once every three months so they could report what was happening and then coordinate their future efforts. He probably took this idea from his knowledge of Quaker organisation. Thus was born the concept of Quarterly Meetings, which were to be central to Methodist organisation until the 1970s. Bennet held the very first two, one for Lancashire at Todmarton on 18 October and one for Cheshire at Woodley on 20 October.

On her return to the Orphan House, Grace rested for a week but during that time she faced a storm of criticism for having travelled with Wesley. Many saw her conduct as unseemly:

'Till now I had received all things, honour or dishonour, the good will or ill will of any, as from the hand of God. But now I began to think, 'How hard is this?' To use me thus? After I have slaved for them for so many years? Well, I will get out of it all. I

---

183 7 October 1749 letter to Thomas Bigg in Newcastle, given in full in W. Stamp, The Orphan House of Wesley, J. Mason 1863 pg 52

will leave them to themselves. I will suffer this no longer.' By this means I was fretted and weakened, and was brought to think of what I had before cast far from me.'[184]

It was perhaps with some relief she undertook a preaching tour:

'I visited all the societies in the south, settled the bands, and endeavoured to remove offences, and regulate all things as well as I could. I then went the north round, and stayed a week at Berwick. I was very ill when I came there. Two days I stayed within, and many came to me. The third night... I earnestly besought God to show me for what end he had brought me to that place? It was then impressed on my mind, to meet the class of children, which I accordingly did the next morning. As soon as I began to sing, the power of God was upon us and increased more and more... [Some of the children] walk in the light to this day.'[185]

In this context it is worth saying that encouraging the faith of children was judged a vital part of any Methodist leader's role.[186] Years later Wesley was to say to one female class leader that she must expect to undertake a double role with the young. She not only had to help the children who had been converted to grow spiritually but she had also 'to watch over the new-born babes... who had 'not yet either much light or much strength.' [187]

Wesley, of course, refused permission for Bennet to marry

---

184 JWLL pg 58

185 JWLL pg 60

186 John Wesley had benefitted hugely from the education he had received from his mother and so it was natural for him to encourage women to take educational initiatives. Famous examples include the work in schools of Molly Maddern in Kingswood, Mary Bishop in Bath and of Mary Bosanquet and Sarah Ryan in Leytonstone.

187 Letter to Hester Ann Roe Rogers 9 Dec 1781 in J. Telford, Letters of JW, Epworth 1931 Vol VII pg 96

Grace: 'My consent I cannot, dare not give. Nor I fear can God give you his blessing.'[188] He said he did not blame the preacher for wanting to marry Grace but Bennet needed to know that she was already promised to him and that this was the will of God. The letter included an explanation of why Grace had not been able to say anything about her engagement to him. Simultaneously Wesley wrote to Grace to say she could put her conscience at rest. Bennet had no prior claim because no preacher could offer marriage without first getting clearance and Bennet had not done that. It followed therefore that anything he had said to her was invalid and so was anything she had said in reply. As in his letter to Bennet, he said it was God's will that she should marry him and not Bennet.

As far as Wesley was concerned, these two letters should have closed the matter, but they did not. Bennet still strongly felt he had the prior claim and said so. At first Wesley wrongly presumed the preacher's refusal to accept his judgement could only have one cause – that Bennet had already married Grace, but Bennet quickly explained this was not the case. He made clear that neither he nor Grace had ever contemplated marrying without Wesley's permission. As far as Grace was concerned, she was not able to accept Wesley's argument that Bennet's original talk of marriage had possessed absolutely no validity. Wesley was later to say that her confusion on this issue was the origin of the disaster that stuck them:

'Hence I date her fall: here was the first false step, which God permitted indeed, but not approved. I was utterly amazed.'[189]

Bennet's constant reiteration that God wanted her to marry him left Grace totally confused. John Wesley was later to write of her

188 JWLL pg 191
189 JWLL pg 2

'racking uncertainty' that autumn and winter as she was in receipt of letters from both him and Bennet:

'When she received a letter from me, she resolved to live and die with me, and wrote to me just what she felt. When she heard from him, her affection for him revived, and she wrote to him in the tenderest manner.'[190]

Some historians have criticised Grace for simply not telling one of the two men to go away and it has even been suggested she enjoyed playing them off against each other. That ignores the fact that she was dealing with two strong-minded men who were both declaring with total conviction they knew best what God wanted her to do.

It also does not take into account that, from a lover's viewpoint, neither John Wesley nor John Bennet were behaving sensibly. It is obvious that both men thought their preaching duties and the needs of the revival overrode all else and therefore neither moved quickly to resolve the situation. In the limited correspondence that has survived between them they seem to write more about preaching commitments than anything else. A letter sent by John to Bennet on 25 November, for example, is mainly about asking Bennet to extend his preaching into Yorkshire and Lincolnshire and one sent on 9 January 1749 is devoted to asking Bennet to take over visiting all the societies that until then had been led by William Darnay.[191] The truth is that neither man wanted to upset the other. Bennet looked on Wesley as his mentor and spiritual master. Wesley looked on Bennet as one of his most effective preachers and one who was central to the work in the north. He recognised that, if he really upset Bennet,

---

190 JWLL pg 3

191 Darnay's Calvinist views were so strong that he had refused to submit to Wesley's control. Another letter from John to Bennet in February 1749 asks him to defend Methodism against the charge that it was supportive of the behaviour of a Moravian preacher then on trial. He describes Bennet as being 'the most proper person of all others' to do it. Letter is in J B's letter book pg 41 John Rylands Library.

he might risk not only losing his services but also endangering his relationship with most of the preachers who had worked with him. This included a number of his leading preachers, including Thomas Richards, one of the first five of Wesley's sons of the gospel, William Shent, a wigmaker from Leeds, Robert Swindells, a convert from Bennet's work in Cheshire, Christopher Hopper, the farmer's son from County Durham that Grace had encouraged to preach, and Thomas Colbeck and Paul Greenwood, both from Keighley in Yorkshire.

What this meant was that Grace was left in a kind of limbo. Both men wrote to her to reiterate they loved her and that they had God on their side, and yet neither of them visited her or showed any urgency about resolving the question of whom she should marry. What made her situation worse was that she could not seek advice from a third party because she had promised not to say anything about her situation to anyone. Although John Wesley would have liked Grace to have just accepted he was totally right and Bennet was totally wrong on the issue of what God wanted, he certainly was not condemnatory of her behaviour at this time because he recognised she was desperate not to betray or displease either him or Bennet:

'One cannot excuse her behaviour in all this time: doubtless she should have renounced one or the other. But those who know human nature will pity her much, at least as much as they will blame her.'[192]

The unresolved claim of Bennet on Grace and the uncertainty that created may possibly help explain why John Wesley said nothing about his hopes of marrying Grace to his brother when Charles finally summed up the courage to tell John about his love for Sally

192 JWLL pg 4

Gwynne in November 1748. To Charles' surprise, John did not reiterate all the arguments about it being inappropriate for either of them to marry. Instead he simply objected to Charles' choice. He said that Sally's age and aristocratic upbringing made her unsuitable. We do not have John's exact words but they were probably similar to what he told one of his preachers who wanted to marry a young wife:

> '[She] will not do: not only as she is far too young, little more than a child, but as she only has little, if any, Christian experience. You want a woman of middle age, well-tried, of good sense, and of deep experience'. [193]

From John's perspective, there was no question but that Sally Gwynne would hinder rather than help Charles serve God. She had played no significant role in the work of the revival and her background made it unlikely that she ever would. She would not wish to travel the country or personally engage in leading classes or speaking to societies or visiting the sick and dying, especially in the slum areas of the towns and cities in which they worked. He told his brother it would be far better for him to choose a woman with a proven track record, someone like Sarah Perrin, the housekeeper at the New Room. It is hard not to see in this John justifying in his own mind his selection of Grace as his potential wife. The social discrepancy between the backgrounds of Grace and Sally may, of course, have been a factor in why John did not choose at this point to tell Charles about his love for Grace. What would Sally – or indeed his brother – think of having a former servant as a potential sister-in-law? Grace's relatively humble origin did not matter to John but

---

193 JW to a shopkeeper called Thomas Mason. 30 May 1771, Proceedings of Wesley Hist. Society 1906 pg 283

he knew it would matter to many others and having wives from such disparate backgrounds was hardly likely to be straightforward for the brothers. What makes John's silence about his feelings for Grace remarkable is that he had a reputation for being very open – indeed Charles once said his brother could never keep secrets since he was born. It is a gift God has not given him'![194] On this occasion he was definitely wrong!

Although John did not inform Charles about his relationship with Grace, that relationship clouded his response to his brother's proposed marriage. For example, when Charles said that John would have to create some financial provision for him so he could afford to marry, John resisted the idea, in part because he thought the Methodist movement could ill afford to pay for the upkeep of two wives. Knowing how modestly Grace was prepared to live, he told Charles that Sally required a lifestyle that was too costly. This is not quite as harsh as it sounds because the Gwynnes wanted a guaranteed annuity in Sally's name of £100 per year.[195] To achieve that required an investment of £2,500 and that money had to come from the sale of publications. The scale of this is best understood if one recalls that the cost of adapting the Foundery in London for Methodist use had been just £700. John only retracted his refusal to agree to Charles' marriage after Charles threatened to cease his role in the revival in order to earn a salary through becoming a parish priest.

The experience of dealing with John's hostility on the issue of his choice of wife confirmed in Charles' mind that his brother would never marry. He and his friend, George Whitefield, agreed that this was probably a good thing given John's key role in the revival.

194 Cited John Whitehead, Life of Rev JW, London 1793 Vol II pg 389

195 Sally's mother, Mrs Gwynne, had made it a condition of giving her approval for the wedding that Charles had at least this level of income so that her daughter would be living with a reasonable degree of financial stability.

However, the public announcement of Charles' forthcoming wedding brought an end to the policy of telling the lay preachers that they should remain single. One example will suffice to illustrate that. At this time John Wesley's right hand man was the preacher John Jones and he had just appointed him as chief master of the newly opened Kingswood School. Jones – like the other five teachers appointed – had vowed to stay single and devote their energies entirely to the school, which Wesley had created to fulfil a double role. It would be the place to which the lay preachers would go to study and it would create the next generation of preachers by providing a Christian education for the children of his friends.[196] John Jones, immediately after he heard the news of Charles' engagement, visited London in order to propose to Elizabeth Mann, a class leader at the Foundery and they were married on 8 February 1749. John Wesley officiated.

By that time John Wesley had determined in his own mind how he was going to resolve the issue of whom Grace should marry. He would take her with him on his next planned tour of Ireland and that would enable God to show whether he wanted them to marry or not.[197] It would also, of course, give him the advantage over Bennet, who would not be able to influence her thinking. He therefore ordered her to leave Newcastle and join up with him at Kingswood School. He said she could leave her son Jackey, the child by her previous marriage, as one of its pupils whilst she accompanied him as his servant to Ireland. Grace wrote to Bennet to say she was travelling southwards in March in response to a summons by Wesley, and, if he truly loved her, he should meet her in Sheffield before she did what Wesley asked. Unfortunately a family bereavement prevented Bennet responding to her plea. His brother-

---

196 By friends Wesley meant those people who were supporting Methodism, not just his personal friends.

197 The very fact that John saw Ireland as a means of checking that Grace was the right potential choice has led some historians to suggest that his initial offer of marriage may not have been as clear cut as his account makes out and that this was why Grace had not yet turned away Bennet. She really did not know whether John's words on their possible marriage was no more than just talk.

in-law had unexpectedly died and so he did not get to Sheffield in time. Unaware of why Bennet had failed to see her, Grace moved on to Bristol. John had arrived there on 22 February and based himself mainly at Kingswood School.[198]

The timing cannot have been easy for Grace because she was arriving in Bristol literally less than a fortnight before the date set for Charles Wesley's marriage to Sally Gwynne. Was it coincidence or not that on 1 April John unexpectedly announced to Charles that he had severe doubts about giving his brother permission to marry the aristocratic Sally? [199] This was said literally on the Saturday morning that he and Charles were supposed to be heading off to Wales to go to the Gwynne's family home at Garth prior to the wedding on 8 April. John refused to leave Kingswood School that day. Charles in his journal says: 'I kept my temper.'[200] Few brothers would. The ostensible reason given for John's change of mind was that he was averse to signing the financial agreement that he had promised because it involved handing over the profits for over sixty of their published works.

Wesley spent some of the 2 April writing a letter to John Bennet. It has not survived, but from Bennet's reply (written on 25 April), some of its contents can be implied. Its general gist was that Bennet had broken his promise to do nothing without John's consent, that he had tried to marry Grace behind Wesley's back, that he was being driven by his desire to get a wife rather than by any specific love

---

198 He held a training course at the school for seventeen of the lay preachers on 23 and 24 March and then embarked on a variety of preaching engagements within the Bristol circuit.

199 A possible trigger for John's action, other than concern over the disparity between the social backgrounds of Grace and Sally, may have been the opposition that was being expressed by some of the Methodist members to Charles' choice of wife. On 6 March Charles had held a meeting with 'a select band' of people in Bristol to talk about his forthcoming marriage. They said Sally was an inappropriate choice for a wife because of the income required to maintain the kind of lifestyle to which she had become accustomed. Charles had angrily told them that he desired 'their prayers not their advice', but they almost certainly would have lobbied John on the issue. Only George Whitefield seems to have been truly happy about Charles marrying Sally.

200 CWJ 1 April 1749

for Grace, and that he was not obeying what God wanted. Bennet's response is an interesting one. First and foremost, he made quite clear that it was never his intention to marry someone without first notifying and consulting Wesley and that he was a most loyal follower:

> 'I believe you to be a minister of Christ, an elder of the Church, and account you worthy of double honour; and desire that I may both in this affair and all others show that reverence and obedience to you which is suitable in young ones towards their elders.'

All he asked John to do was to recognise that it was not reasonable to expect him to regard anyone as being infallible and to do things that ran counter to his conscience:

> 'You desire I may speak to you without reserve, therefore I would speak freely whatever is in my heart... Our letters, I must acknowledge, have puzzled me, so that I have not seen clearly the will of God. I never intended to marry until both she and I have seen you face to face. I assure you I do not want a woman. If so, I needed not to have acquainted you and given you so much trouble. I thought (and still think) that it will be more for the glory of God was I to marry. I am at present resigned. And I trust shall not act imprudently. I can say only this: I would rather die than bring a reproach upon the gospel.'

The most fascinating part of the letter is its conclusion. Bennet wrote that the problem they were in had arisen out of John's mistaken views on the subject of marriage. It was these that had led people 'into strange errors'. He said John should be more aware of the problems facing Grace. She was a woman who wanted to get married and who was constantly being tempted to do so because, as a preacher, she was always in the company of men. She had not got married because she knew that John disapproved of anyone involved in preaching doing so and she wanted to please him, but this was slowly driving her to despair:

> 'Sir, I believe I know as much of GM's weakness and temptations as any one person. She has lost ground and is weaker in grace ever since she appeared publicly. She hath lain under sore temptations, and hath been a snare to others, though not designedly, both teachers and hearers. She is in danger (whether you know it or not) of waxing wanton against Christ, growing weary of the Church service, and by despairing of marrying in the Church, revolt from the faith. If you hurry her from place to place, and thereby she is more and more exposed, until at last her weakness is betrayed, I am free – look you to it. It is against her mind she is gone [on] this journey – more, I believe, to please you than a conviction it is the will of God. Whether ever I see her more in the flesh or not, I desire you will be tender of her character, and consider she is a woman.'[201]

The letter was addressed to the Foundery in London because Bennet was not aware that John was going to Ireland with Grace. By the time he heard what was going on, it was too late for Bennet to make any contact with Grace and he must have resigned himself to the likelihood that he might never see her again. The letter was forwarded to Ireland. Did its contents encourage John Wesley to believe that, if he wanted to marry Grace, he had better make that absolutely clear to her before they returned to England?

---

201 25 April 1749 Ms is in John Rylands Library and entire letter is transcribed in F. Baker, Works of JW, Clarendon Press 1982 Vol 26 pg 351-4

Charles Wesley appears to have thought it was best not to enter into a direct confrontation with John over their delay in going to the Gwynnes. Nevertheless, he did not take kindly to discovering on the Sunday that John had made preaching commitments in Wales that extended until the following Friday, even though Charles had promised they would reach the Gwynne family home in Garth either by the Tuesday or, at the latest, Wednesday. The brothers, accompanied by a travelling companion called William Tucker, and, of course, by Grace, set off on the Monday with Charles understandably feeling, in his words, 'weary, faint,[and] oppressed'.[202] A bad passage to Wales caused John to miss an engagement he had made to preach in Newport and to be late for one at Pedwas, near Caerphilly. On Tuesday he insisted on preaching at Cardiff, Lanmais and Fonmon, where one of John's clerical friends, John Hodges, tried (possibly at Wesley's request) to persuade Charles to abandon the marriage. Charles records that Hodges told him:

'My brother, what are you seeing in this thing? Happiness? Then you will be sadly disappointed.'[203]

On Wednesday John preached at Cowbridge and Lantrissent and on Thursday at Aberdare. Not all of these engagements had been arranged in advance so John was clearly deliberately delaying their arrival in Garth. Although most historians have implied this simply shows John's commitment to his preaching, the engagements can also be seen, as one historian has pointed out, 'as a pointed reminder to Charles as to where his priorities should lie'.[204] On the Thursday evening Charles and John arrived in Brecon where they met with a lawyer, Thomas James, and he arranged for them to obtain from

202 CWJ 3 April 1749
203 CWJ 4 April 1749
204 G. Lloyd, CW and the Struggle for Methodist Identity OUP 2007 pg 97

a local clergyman a marriage licence. They finally got to Garth on the Friday in time for breakfast. However, as John had not signed any financial settlement, it was still uncertain whether the wedding would go ahead. Charles says in his journal that matters were talked over with Mrs Gwynne and she managed to persuade John that his fears about Sally's unsuitability were unfounded. Presumably she reassured John that the Gwynnes would not seek to stop Charles working for the Methodists and that their daughter would fully support the work of the revival. It was only then that John finally gave his assent for the marriage to proceed, signing a bond to confirm that he would on his return from Ireland make a proper financial agreement so Charles could have an agreed income from Methodist book sales.

Grace was at Garth House in the capacity of John's servant and she did not attend the wedding ceremony, which took place at 8.00 a.m on the Saturday in the Llanlleonfel parish church in Garth.[205] John wrote only one sentence in his published journal on the marriage, at which he officiated:

'I married my brother and Sarah Gwynne. It was a solemn day, such as became the dignity of a Christian marriage.'[206]

Charles provides us with more information. He says the wedding party rose at four and he and John spent three and a half hours before the service with Sally and her sister Becky praying and singing hymns. John then led the service with Marmaduke Gwynne giving away his daughter's hand in marriage to Charles. The service included the sacrament of holy communion and all present sang

205 Charles lists as those present Sally's father and her sisters and sister-in-law, Lady Elizabeth Rudd (but interestingly not her mother) and four others: Thomas James, the attorney from Brecon, William Tucker, his brother's travelling companion, Grace Bowen, the family's nurse, and Betty Williams, a friend of the family.

206 JWJ 8 April 1749

'Come thou everlasting Lord', a wedding hymn which had been specially written by Charles. John then gave the couple his blessing. Charles concludes his account by saying 'we were cheerful without mirth, serious without sadness' and that the wedding to an outsider would have looked 'more like a funeral than a wedding'. Was this just the solemnity of the occasion or was this in part because of the series of unhappy events that had preceded the wedding?

Grace, relegated to the status of John's servant, must have contrasted her position with that of the bride, especially hearing Charles talk repeatedly of 'my Sally' and of the pleasure he would have in introducing her to all the religious societies. It is easy to surmise that seeing Charles marry such an aristocratic wife must have made Grace question whether it was right for someone as lowly as her to marry John. But what did the wedding make John feel? The only clue we have is Charles' statement that 'my brother seemed the happiest person among us'.[207] Was this because John was now thinking more seriously about his own forthcoming marriage with Grace or was it simply that, having finally given his permission, he was content to enjoy his brother's marriage? At 4.a.m on Monday 10 April John set off for Holyhead, accompanied by Grace and William Tucker, and they boarded a ship for Ireland five days later. John was now to have the time he wanted to test whether God did really want him to marry Grace.

207 ibid

Kingswood School and Preaching House (from print in the New Room)

John Wesley (from print in the New Room, engraved by J. Andrews)

5

GRACE'S PROMISE TO MARRY JOHN WESLEY

The ten weeks that John Wesley spent in Ireland with Grace Murray considerably strengthened his desire to marry Grace. She continually impressed him by her very active part in his ministry:

'I saw the work of God prosper in her hands. She lightened my burden more than can be expressed. She examined all the women in the smaller societies and the believers in every place. She settled all the women bands, visited the sick, prayed with the mourners, more and more of whom received remission of sins during her conversation or prayer. Meantime she was to me both a servant and a friend, as well as a fellow labourer. She provided everything I wanted. She told me with all faithfulness and freedom if she thought anything amiss in my behaviour. And (what I never saw in any other to this day) she knew how to reconcile the utmost plainness of speech with such deep respect and esteem as I often trembled at, not thinking it was due to any creature…[and she combined this] with the most exquisite modesty, a tenderness not to be expressed. The more we conversed together the more I loved her.'[208]

Yet curiously none of this was conveyed to anyone else, not even his

208 JWLL pg 4-5

brother. John's letters to Charles do not even mention Grace.

Before they left Ireland Wesley put his relationship with Grace onto a new footing by formally agreeing a 'spousal de praesenti'. This meant that they both swore an oath of allegiance to each other. Before the Marriage Act of 1753 it was quite common for people to engage in private marriage contracts.[209] With not a single letter reaching her from Bennet following his failure to see her at Sheffield, it is not surprising that Grace acceded to this. According to Wesley the affair between her and Bennet 'was as if it had never been'.[210] The exact legal status of this 'spousal de praesenti' depended upon the words used. If John and Grace vowed 'I take thee to be...' this was deemed to amount to an unconditional allegiance and this meant the couple were to all intents and purposes legally married. However, if both of the couple swore 'I will take thee...' this implied their vows were subject to certain conditions being met and so it was more a 'spousal de futuro' (i.e. a declaration of intent to marry in the future). Most historians agree the vows made by John and Grace were conditional because both of them agreed to say nothing yet in public about their relationship until John had spoken first to his brother and to John Bennet. If, as is likely, John made it a condition that these men agreed to the marriage, the 'spousal de praesenti' only became legal when that condition was met. The only exception to this was if the parties to the agreement had sexual intercourse. If that happened, then the union rather than meeting the conditions constituted a legal marriage.

It says much for John's determination to exclude Bennet that he undertook such an agreement because the Church did not really approve of this kind of private arrangement – that was partly the

---

209 This Marriage Act required all marriages to take place in the parish church to which one of the couple belonged. It required banns to be read in advance to check there was no obstacle to the union and, after the ceremony, the marriage had to be recorded in the parish register and signed by the couple and witnesses.
210 JWLL pg 5

reason for the Marriage Act of 1753, which ended the practice. The Church preferred people to make a commitment in an open place before witnesses and with the benefit of a presiding clergyman. Presumably from John's perception the 'spousal de paresenti' was a means of securing an oath from Grace that she would be his wife rather than the wife of Bennet until he had undertaken the steps he felt were necessary. What Grace made of the 'spousal de praesenti' is not certain. She may well have not understood her exact legal position but, in the words of one historian, 'it probably sounded good to her, and doubtless she participated in the simple ceremony with proper solemnity and enthusiasm'. [211] John was later to write that as far as both of them were concerned they were now destined for each other:

'Companions now in weal and woe,
No Power on Earth could us divide:
Nor summer's heat, nor wintry snow
Could tear my partner from my side;
Nor toil, nor weariness, nor pain,
Nor horrors of the angry main.

Oft, (tho' as yet the nuptial tie
was not), clasping her hand in mine,
'What force', she said, 'beneath the sky,
Can now our well-knit souls disjoin?
With thee I'd go to India's coast,
To worlds in distant ocean lost!"[212]

When the couple arrived back in Bristol there was no immediate

---

211 F.E. Maser, John Wesley's Only Marriage, Methodist History 1977 Vol 16 pg 34
212 JW's Poem on Grace Murray

opportunity for John to speak with Charles and Sally because the couple happened to be away in London at the time. On 25 July John visited Kingswood School, presumably with Grace, who would have wished to see her son. John was extremely unhappy with what he found at the school because both its teachers and its pupils were ignoring many of his rules. He thought this had arisen largely because he had relaxed the rule about staff entering into relationships. John Jones' wife Elizabeth was proving far more of a handicap than a help to her husband because she loathed living at the school and being surrounded by the Kingswood colliers. John Wesley describes her as being 'fretful, peevish, murmuring, discontented with everything.'[213] Equally he felt the romance between the school's next most senior teacher, Thomas Richards, and the school's housekeeper, Mary Davey, had stopped her focusing on her duties. This may have given John second thoughts about the wisdom of marrying Grace because he made no effort at all to tell Charles about the 'spousal de praesenti' when Charles and Sally arrived in Bristol on the evening of the 26 July. Alternatively he may simply have judged it was correct to speak with John Bennet first so he could obtain his assent.

Whatever the reason for John's silence, Grace was agitated about her invidious position. What alarmed her yet more was that she had heard the staff at Kingswood gossiping about the affection John had shown towards the schoolmistress Molly Francis and heard speculation that he would shortly be marrying her. This sufficiently upset her that she decided to write a letter to Bennet – the first correspondence she had had with him since his failure to meet her in Sheffield. It has been suggested that this was the action of a jealous woman and that Grace would therefore not have coped with Wesley's itinerancy any better than did his eventual wife, Molly Vazeille, who was bitterly suspicious of Wesley's dealings with other women. That

213 Written after Elizabeth Jones' death JWJ 26 Nov 1752

is unfair because Molly's character was totally different from that of Grace and Grace's position at this time was not that of a wife. Grace may have felt some jealousy about Wesley's alleged relationship with Molly Francis, but almost certainly her main response was one of panic that she had pinned her hopes on a marriage with Wesley that was not going to take place. She almost immediately regretted her action in writing to Bennet because the very next day she confessed what she had done to Wesley.

Remarkably Wesley made no effort to head north to see Bennet. Instead, on 1 August, he set off for London with John Jones. Grace was still just functioning in public as his servant. He spent a few days at the Foundery attending to various issues. Grace's continued anxiety probably explains why she broke her promise not to tell anyone about her relationship with him. She confided in a friend, Elizabeth Maxfield[214], and received a distressing response. Elizabeth said the societies would never accept John Wesley marrying a servant, especially as Grace had journeyed with Wesley for months. That would be misinterpreted as her having been his mistress. She told Grace:

'It would never do… the people here would never suffer you. And your proud spirit would not bear their behaviour: you have not humility enough, or meekness, or patience; you would be miserable all your life. If you love yourself or if you love him, never think of it more'.[215]

Unable to share what Elizabeth had told her, Grace's anxiety mounted as she accompanied Wesley and John Jones to the Gywnne's new family home in Ludlow, where they arrived on 7 August.

---

214 The friend is identified only by the initials E.M. but is thought this was most likely Elizabeth Maxfield, the wife of the lay preacher.

215 JWLL pg 6

Charles and Sally joined them there. The purpose of the meeting was to sort out the delayed financial settlement so that Charles could set up a proper home for his wife in Bristol. He had been forced to rent temporary accommodation in the Stokes Croft area of the city and it was totally inappropriate because it was too near the Full Moon Inn, a place where prostitutes employed their trade. Charles and Sally had found it difficult to sleep at night because of the noise of coaches bringing in customers. A proper home had become essential, not least because Sally was showing signs of sickness and this was probably because she was in the very early stages of pregnancy. Seeing the sums required to fund accommodation for his brother and sister-in-law may have further increased John's concern about whether he should also marry. He said nothing about his relationship with Grace to his brother. She was still just there as his servant.

It was not until the end of the month that John finally headed northwards with Grace. They met up with Bennet at Epworth on 31 August. Unfortunately the impact of receiving Grace's letter had been to revive Bennet's hopes. The next day there was a massive confrontation between the two men. According to Bennet:

> 'We had a long dispute and such a contention arose as had never happened with us before. This day I shall remember so long as I have breath.'[216]

According to John, it was only now that he discovered how extensively in the past Grace had been in communication with Bennet. What especially annoyed him was that she had dared to copy some of his letters for the preacher to see. We can only speculate as to why she had done this. Was it, as some assert, that she enjoyed playing the

---

216 1 Sept 1749 JBD pg 194

men of against each other and wanted to make Bennet jealous? Or was it done to cure Bennet of his passion by making him realise how much John loved her and how there was little chance that the preacher would win Wesley's permission to marry Grace? Or did she hope Bennet might be persuaded by the arguments that Wesley was using in his correspondence about God having prepared her to become his wife? Whatever the reason for her action, it left John feeling both confused and enraged. How could she have dared to copy some of his intimate correspondence so that Bennet could read it? His jealousy at her obvious close relationship with Bennet made him declare the true depth of his own passion, but, after sleeping on the matter, he judged it right to send Grace a letter the next morning saying she should marry Bennet without delay.

Understandably Grace was devastated, not least because she regarded the 'spousal de praesenti' as a real commitment. Wesley says that she ran to him 'in an agony of tears' and begged him to reconsider his decision lest he kill her. Her expressions of love distressed him 'exceedingly', and, as he was struggling to regain control of his emotions, Bennet broke in upon them and 'claimed her as his right'.[217] Wesley gives the strangest of justifications for what he did next. He says that he felt in his heart that Grace must prefer Bennet and so, rather than upset her further, he determined 'to give her up' because he loved her too much to cause her further pain. He therefore left her with Bennet and returned to his lodgings alone:

'I felt no anger, no murmuring, no repining; but deep anguish of spirit from a piercing conviction of the irreparable loss I had sustained. I had no desire to converse with her anymore'. [218]

217 JWLL pg 7
218 JWLL pg 7-8

The next day news was brought to him that Grace had taken to her bed 'exceedingly ill'. He therefore went to see her:

> 'When I came, she told me in [no uncertain] terms, 'My dear sir, how can you possibly think I love any one better than I love you! I love you a thousand times better than I ever loved John Bennet in my life.'[219]

Grace then expressed her fear that, if she rejected Bennet, he might go mad. John says this was not just her imagination because 'she showed me a letter he had just sent her which confirmed that fear.'[220]

One would think that with all this drama going on the last thing on the minds of Wesley and Bennet would have been their preaching commitments, but that was not the case. True to his vow to put God first, Wesley chose to leave Grace alone in order to go and preach. That evening Bennet arrived to see her, bringing the preacher David Trathen in support. The two men urged her to turn her back on Wesley and Bennet says in his diary: 'The dispute somewhat ended in favour of me.'[221] According to what Grace later told Wesley, the two men refused to leave her room until she had solemnly promised to marry Bennet rather than him. Once he had secured this promise, Bennet then did as Wesley had done: he left Grace so he could head off to Sheffield to undertake his preaching commitments.

When John returned from his preaching on 3 September Grace told him what had happened during his absence but he did not respond well to the news that she had let herself be forced into agreeing to marry Bennet. For three days they travelled northwards together. Wesley wrote of that journey: 'I was perplexed.... I knew

219 JWLL pg 8
220 ibid
221 JBD pg 194

not whether I ought to let her go… I was utterly unresolved.'[222] It ran against John's nature to be decisive in this situation. Despite all his outward determination, he was at times deeply unsure of himself as the historian Augustin Leger pointed out after he transcribed John's account of events:

> 'Inflexible as his opinions commonly were, it is true few men have shown more distrust of their own judgement, more humility and docility to the guidance of others than Wesley did… He describes himself as 'fearful of trusting his own judgement.'[223]

Although there were certain principles from which Wesley never departed, over the years he had always looked for advice from someone that he was doing the right thing. In his early years it had been to his mother, as a student to various writers like William Law, as a young presbyter to the Moravians, and so on. He often wrote to those he regarded as his friends, asking them for guidance or their opinions:

> 'I want more light, more strength for my personal walking with God, and I know not but how he may give it me through you.'[224]

It was his constant readjusting of his views in the light of what others said that led one of Wesley's critics to say:

> '[He] is the veriest weathercock that ever was; he has not wit enough to be fixed in anything, but is tossed to and fro continually… No two disputants… can be more opposite to

---

222 JWLL pg 8
223 JWLL pg 198
224 16 Sept 1757 to Rev. Samuel Walker of Truro in Works (1872 edition) Vol XIII pg 204

each other than he is to himself'.[225]

On this occasion there was no one to whom he could look for advice on how to disentangle the mess he found himself in.

On the evening of 6 September they reached the outskirts of Newcastle and Wesley finally made his decision. He told Grace that he would not force her to marry Bennet – he would let her choose whom she should marry. This type of volte-face was not untypical of him.[226] He says her response was immediate: 'I am determined by conscience, as well as by inclination, to live and die with you.'[227] The next day Wesley wrote to Bennet a not very gracious letter, accusing him of a gross betrayal of trust and of seeking to rob him of a highly valued servant:

'My dear brother, the friendship between you and me has continued long. I pray it may continue to our lives' ends. But, if I love you, I must deal plainly with you, and surely you desire that I should.... Oh that you would consider what I say with meekness and love and with continual prayer to God!.... As one of my helpers, I desired you, three years ago, to assist me in Newcastle. In my house there I placed a servant whom I had tried several years, and found faithful in all things. Therefore I trusted her in the highest degree, and put her in the highest office that any woman can bear among us. Both by the nature and rules of your office you were engaged to do nothing of importance without consulting me. She was likewise engaged.... to take no step of any moment without my knowledge and consent....

225 Richard Hill and responded to by Wesley in Some Remarks on Mr Hill's Review in Works (1872 edition) Vol X pg 377

226 A number of contemporaries comment on John's occasional ability to dramatically change his mind. See section on difficulties of assessing John's true character in H. D. Rack, Reasonable Enthusiast, Epworth 1989, pg 535-550.

227 JWLL pg 9

Notwithstanding this, you were scarce out of my house when, without consulting me, you solicited her to take a step of the last importance.... You, whom I had trusted in all things, thus betrayed your trust and moved her to do so too. You, to whom I had done no wrong, wronged me.... You endeavoured to rob me of a faithful and most useful servant, the fellow to whom, for the work committed to her care, I know not where to find in the three kingdoms.'

He then went on to say how he had come to love Grace and realised that it was God's will they should marry and how Bennet was grossly interfering:

'Last autumn I observed her more narrowly and perceived she was such a person as I had sought for many years, and then determined never to part with her. I told her this but.... [said] I could do nothing without consulting my brother.... I told her.... 'I am convinced it is not the will of God that you should be shut up in a corner. I am convinced you ought to labour with me in the gospel. I therefore design to take you to Ireland in the spring.'..... And from that time I looked upon her as my own, and resolved that nothing but death should part us. Three days after I left her.... you solicited her again. And in a few days more prevailed upon her to imply and promise marriage to you.... Upon her return from Ireland.... you rushed out and by vehement importunity forced her tender and compassionate mind to promise you again.... Was not all this quite unjust and unkind? As well as treacherous and unfaithful?.... Was this consistent either with gratitude or friendship? Nay, with common justice or humanity?'

Wesley finished by saying that, as far as he was concerned, any promise Grace had made to Bennet was null and void and so he could never look for Wesley to bless his marriage to her:

'I doubt still whether a thousand promises can bind to a thing evil and wrong in itself.... I can say no more – only this – you may tear her away by violence, but my consent I cannot, dare not give. Nor I fear can God give you his blessing.'[228]

Grace also wrote to Bennet but all she said was that she had sinned in agreeing to marry him without first having obtained Wesley's consent and it was God's will she should marry Wesley. Both letters were given to the lay preacher William Shent to deliver to Bennet.

Only now did John think it was time to tell his brother about Grace. He sent a copy of his letter to Bennet to Charles in Bristol. He then set about his normal preaching duties, taking Grace with him on a tour of the northern societies. That included visiting Morpeth, Alnwick and Berwick on Tweed and he felt 'every hour gave me fresh proof of her usefulness on the one hand and of her affection on the other'.[229] They spent five days in Berwick, much of the time in prayer, and Wesley spent a couple of the evenings copying out an account that Grace had written about her life and her spiritual journey. It seemed to make him even more certain that she would be the perfect wife for him. All the problems that she had faced in her life were evidence of God's desire to prepare her for her marriage to him. God had fed her with the 'bread of adversity' and the 'water of affliction' so that she could become 'a comforter of many, a Mother in Israel.' [230] After this time spent together, Grace told him:

'In times past I could have married another, if you would have

228 JWLL pg 9-14
229 JWLL pg 14
230 JWLL pg 15. 'A Mother in Israel' is a reference to Deborah, the only female prophet in the Bible.

given me away, but now it is impossible we should part. God has united us forever.'

He and Grace arrived back in Newcastle on Saturday 16 September. After a busy day on Sunday, they talked late into the night and Grace gave him 'all the assurances which words could give of the most intense and inviolable affection.' [231]

Despite this account of mutual love, all was still not straightforward for Grace because John refused to fix a wedding day. He said she could not expect him to do that until he had first done three things. The first was to obtain his brother Charles' consent. Although this was perhaps a reasonable request, she must have felt he had had plenty of opportunities to do that and not done so. The second action that Wesley felt was required was for him to satisfy John Bennet that it was right for them to marry – something that Grace knew was impossible. The third was to send an account of John's reasons for marrying her to every helper and every society in England with a request for their prayers. This is particularly interesting condition. John often liked to present himself as a man who cared little about public opinion, but he was not unmindful of people's views on propriety. There can be no doubt that Wesley desperately wanted others to give his desire for Grace a stamp of approval. But Grace must have asked herself whether John truly loved her if he had to justify marrying her to everyone – and what if the societies protested? Would he have the courage to marry her regardless?

Just as worrying from Grace's perspective was John's determination to investigate the reasons why some of the women in Newcastle were saying bad things about her. His comment that this was necessary 'to form a clearer judgement of her real character' was

---

231 JWLL pg 61

hardly flattering. [232] Had she not given him proof of her character week after week during all their travels together? When John began questioning her critics, he uncovered a host of petty accusations that were without substance and, in some cases, almost laughable. He says he knew from his own experience that much of what he was told was untrue. For example, there were accusations that Grace wasted money on expensive clothes and, having seen what she wore, John knew that was patently false. There was only one conclusion he could draw:

> 'I plainly perceived jealousy and envy were the real ground of most of these accusations, and idle, senseless prejudice of the rest.... Her character appeared untouched.'[233]

It says much about Grace's concern at John's behaviour that she issued him with an ultimatum. She told him she was not prepared to wait more than a year to marry him. Following this, Wesley confided the secret of his engagement to the lay preacher Christopher Hopper and, at Grace's request, asked him to witness a renewal of the contract they had made in Ireland. If the original agreement had been more of a 'spousal de futuro' than a 'spousal de praesenti', this second occasion was definitely more formal. The wording was based on the marriage ceremony from the Prayer Book.[234] It has been argued that the ceremony was sufficiently formal for it to invalidate the subsequent marriages of Grace to John Bennet and John to Molly Vazeille. However, that is not the case. John was still saying he could not marry Grace until he had won the assent of his brother

---

232 JWLL pg 61

233 JWLL pg 62. John's account provides the name of some of her accusers – Sister Lyddel, Nancy and Peggy Watson, Ann Mattison, Betty Graham, and Mrs Williams, The only man mentioned is Mrs William's husband (and he was possibly dragged into that by his wife).

234 Grace later referred to the fact that 'whom God hath joined together no man can put asunder'.

and of John Bennet and so the agreement was still fundamentally a 'spousal de futuro'. The ceremony therefore, however like a wedding, was not one. It may well have been John's way of reassuring Grace that, despite the long delay in marrying her, he still intended to do so – a gesture to quieten her growing concern that he would never honour his earlier promise. It also meant, of course, that he had once more secured Grace's oath to marry him and not Bennet.

The renewal of the 'spousal de praesenti' took place on 21 September in the village of Hindley Hill, where Christoher Hopper had taken up residence and created a religious society. During this ceremony Hopper noticed that Grace was trembling and he asked her if she had reservations about committing herself to Wesley. Before she could reply, John intervened. He said that if she had the least scruple about marrying him, they should not proceed. Her response was unequivocal: 'I have none at all'. [235] Despite her response, some historians have interpreted her trembling as evidence that she really wanted to marry Bennet and was undergoing the 'spousal de praesenti' under emotional duress. It is far more likely that it was just a product of her emotion at going through this ceremony with the man she loved, especially after all the uncertainties that had preceded it.

Following this second 'spousal de praesenti', John asked Hopper to go and visit Bennet with instructions that he should persuade him to accept that Grace should now marry Wesley. Hopper left but, as far as we know, he took Bennet's side on this issue, believing that John's actions were wrong. Wesley left Hindley Hill almost immediately after Hopper had departed in order to head for Whitehaven and undertake various preaching commitments. He instructed Grace 'to examine and settle the women bands in Allendale' and he wrote of their leave-taking:

235 JWLL pg 63

'I had not one uneasy thought, believing God would give us to meet again at the time when he saw good'.[236]

Grace was clearly fearful that Bennet might ride to Newcastle and create a scene. She therefore sent a letter to her assistant at the Orphan House, asking her to send her warning should Bennet arrive unexpectedly:

'I must not see him. It will tear my soul to pieces seeing I can by no means help him now. For whom God hath joined together no man can put asunder and well I am assured that it was his will it should be so'.[237]

What Grace did not realise was that the real challenge to her marrying John would not come from Bennet but from Charles Wesley.

236 ibid
237 JWLL pg 89

The Orphan House in Newcastle (from print in the New Room)

Charles Wesley (from print in the New Room based on portrait by William Gush)

6

CHARLES WESLEY'S
INTERVENTION

Charles' journal entries cease on 15 September and it is thought he must have received the copy of John's letter to Bennet shortly after that date. What it contained came as a total bombshell. He knew Grace had many qualities but his brother had never given any prior intimation that he wanted to marry her. He saw the letter to Bennet as evidence of a temporary infatuation and, knowing his brother's capacity to idealise women whom he thought he loved, Charles was understandably deeply concerned. This is not as unreasonable a supposition as some have implied. It is worth quoting in this context what John wrote about himself:

'I will tell you how it was with me. Though I do not know I was ever low-spirited (my spirits being always the same, whether in sickness or health), yet I was often uneasy. Even in vigorous health, in plenty, and in the midst of friends, I wanted something; I was not satisfied. I looked about for happiness, but could not find it. Then I thought, 'O, if I had such a person with me, I should surely be happy'. I mused with myself, 'How lovely is her look! How agreeably she talks!.... Surely this is the very thing I want; and, could I attain it, I should then no more be solitary!.... Therefore, with her I can be happy; without her I never can.'[238]

238 A Thought Upon Marriage 1785 in Works (1872 edition) Vol XI pg 464

Charles knew Grace well, having acted as her spiritual mentor, and he did not think she was a sensible choice for his brother. It is possible that this was partly because he had some reservations about Grace's character, because she was prone to be highly emotional at times, but two other reasons are far more obvious. First, she had made a prior promise to marry someone else and John would be accused of stealing her away from Bennet. This was a preacher whom Charles liked and one who deserved better treatment. Secondly, there would be a social scandal if John married a woman who had acted as his servant. Some historians have suggested it was Charles' wife Sally who instigated this opinion because she was horrified at hearing she was to have such a low-born woman as her sister-in-law. There is no evidence for this, although it is likely Sally would have been shocked by the news of what her brother-in-law was intending to do. The truth is that Charles needed no urging from anyone to know that many society members would disapprove.

From previous experience Charles knew more than anyone else how prone John was to get his relationships with women badly wrong. He understood, in the words of one historian, that John was 'a woman-worshipper' and had a 'natural susceptibility to whatever was graceful and amiable in women, especially if united to mental vigour and moral excellence'.[239] He therefore immediately rode northwards to put an end to what he saw as another instance of his brother's folly. His conversations with people on that journey only served to increase his alarm. At Leeds he talked with various preachers, including William Shent and Robert Swindells. They made no bones of the fact they thought his brother was acting very badly in seeking to marry a woman who already belonged to another man. He was effectively pulling rank on Bennet and it was therefore highly likely that, if John actually did marry Grace, many

239 J.H. Rigg, The Living Wesley (2nd edition) Kelly 1891 pg 62-3

preachers would turn against him. They would no longer wish to work for the Wesleyan branch of Methodism. This was extremely worrying because of Bennet's strong links with a number of the preachers, including John Nelson, Thomas Colbeck, John Trembath, Joseph Cownley, Samuel Larwood, John Haughton, David Tratham, Thomas Meyrick and John Maddern, as well as with some of the preachers known as 'Mr Grimshaw's men', such as William Darney, Paul Greenwood, and Jonathan Maskew. Charles feared all the achievements of the past five years were at risk.

Charles moved on with William Shent to Newcastle. There he heard a huge amount of tittle-tattle about Grace from her enemies. According to John Wesley the lead protagonist in this was a woman called Jane Keith, who was jealous of Grace. This woman, whose nickname was 'Holy Mary', told Charles that his brother was in love 'beyond all sense and reason' and that 'all the town was in uproar and all the societies ready to fly in pieces'.[240] This is not the first time that we hear of Jane Keith's animosity towards Grace. She was resident in the Orphan House and the previous autumn John had written her a letter in which he had challenged her hostile attitude and asked her to be 'as one soul' with Grace. Parts of her reply on that occasion are quite revealing:

'I know of nothing amiss betwixt sister M[urray] and me, but we cannot be as one soul (as you express it) for you know she must have a little pre-eminence. I am exceeding willing that she should, and so we live in great peace, and, I believe, in love. You may expect plain dealing from me… I may possibly deal too openly with others… I do not complain that God has not made

---

240 JWLL pg 65

me some fine thing, to be set up to be gazed at.'[241]

The letter, ostensibly to show that there was no hostility on her part, makes out that Grace was interested only in her own standing.

Jane Keith told Charles that Grace was not what she seemed. She said the housekeeper should never have been permitted to accompany his brother because she had used the opportunity to ensnare him, just as she had ensnared others. If John married such an immoral woman, then it was obvious there could only be one outcome. The societies would reject John's leadership and the religious revival would come to an untimely and unhappy end. With his fears thus substantiated, Charles judged he should act quickly to put a stop to John's infatuation. If Grace was to marry anyone, it had to be Bennet and not his brother. He knew he could not rely on others to make John see sense. Only he, as John's brother, would have the power to make him listen to uncomfortable truths.

Charles caught up with John at Whitehaven on 23 September. By then John says that he had already experienced a presentiment that God might not let him marry Grace. He had experienced a dream at night in which Bennet had told him Grace was now with him in Derbyshire. This dream was sufficiently unsettling that John next morning wrote to Grace a letter which began with the lines: 'There is I know not what of sad presage that tells me we shall never meet again'. [242] In subsequent private devotions John says the Biblical text that came 'as a sword' to his heart was 'Son of man, behold I take from the desire of thine eyes with a stroke!'[243] It is very difficult to

---

241 1 Nov 1748 to JW in Arminian Magazine 1779 pg 42-4. John probably published it because of a passage in the letter where Jane writes of herself: 'I work out of choice, having never yet learned how long a woman can remain idle and innocent. I have had as blessed times in my soul sitting at work as ever I had in my life; especially in the night time, when I see nothing but the light of a candle and a white cloth, hear nothing but the sound of my breath, with God in my sight and heaven in my soul'.

242 JWLL pg 63

243 JWLL pg 64

know how to interpret this. One possibility is that the 'presentiment' reflects that John was still experiencing inner conflict about whether it was right for him to marry. This would make even more sense of Grace's concern about whether he ever would really marry her. She would have known of his continued concern on this issue. His statement that 'God wants you to marry me' was perhaps said as much to try and convince himself as her.

Charles told John that love had blinded him and presented him with what he believed to be three truths, however unpalatable his brother found them to be. The first was that the preachers and societies would never accept that it was right for him to marry a woman who had been a servant. In John's account of what Charles said, he says: 'The thought of my marrying... one so lowborn, appeared above measure shocking to him.'[244] This comment has sometimes been interpreted as showing that Charles had become a snob through marrying an aristocratic wife. However, Charles was only repeating what had been said to him in Newcastle and what Elizabeth Maxfield had told Grace months before in London. Her status opened the floodgates to all kinds of accusations about what she and John had been doing together in Ireland. Secondly, Charles reiterated that Grace was already promised to another man. He told John that the preachers would accuse him of riding roughshod over the feelings of her fiancé John Bennet and, in effect, of abusing his role as their leader. Many would cease to accept his authority and this would destroy all that they had achieved. Thirdly, Charles almost certainly stated that the proposed marriage was the product of no more than a temporary infatuation. It ran counter to all that John had publicly proclaimed about the necessity of his remaining single in order to have no personal distractions. Charles may well have listed other women to whom John had made promises of marriage

244 JWLL pg 64

and whom he had not then married.[245]

A number of historians have said that Charles should have been more open to letting his brother marry the woman of his choice, regardless of whether that was good or not for the Methodist movement:

'There is something unpleasing about the spectacle of the happily married brother straining every nerve to stop John following suit on the plea it would damage the connexion. No such calculation had apparently ever concerned him in his own case.'[246]

Others have speculated that there must have been personal factors behind Charles' objections. Was he concerned, for example, that his brother would undertake less itinerant work once he was married and therefore expect Charles to do more? This seems unlikely given John's determination not to let anything hinder his work and Grace's willingness to support the revival. Was Charles worried instead about the possible impact of John's marriage on his financial position? This is a possibility. John was mainly relying on the income from his Oxford fellowship but that fellowship was dependent upon him remaining single. Without it he would have to rely on money from the sale of Methodist publications – the same pot from which Charles relied for his income. However, it is difficult to envisage mercenary motives driving Charles, especially given his love for John. A more likely influence was that Charles strongly believed that John was not cut out by temperament to make anyone a good husband. He knew from his own experience that John expected Sally to make no demands whatsoever on his own time. How much more would he expect of Grace? And what if she had children? John

245 In a secret passage in his journal on 22 March 1751 Charles refers to John acknowledging that he had made promises to the schoolteacher Molly Francis and to a woman from London called Miss Lundy.
246 H. Rack, Reasonable Enthusiast, Epworth (third edition) 2002 pg 264

would see them entirely as encumbrances. When their sister Patty's children had died, John had written:

'I believe the death of your children is a great instance of the goodness of God towards you. You have often mentioned to me how much of your time they took up. Now that time is restored to you, and you have nothing to do but to serve the Lord without carefulness and distraction.' [247]

As far as Charles was concerned, Grace would have a far better and more considerate partner in John Bennet than she ever would in his brother, whose driven nature made him totally unsuited to a married lifestyle. This was probably true. Some of the reasons why John's subsequent marriage to Molly Vazeille failed would have applied just as much if he had married Grace.

That evening John sat down to think about what his brother had said. As the historian Henry Rack has noted, John was 'singularly free of prejudice about status'[248] and so he rapidly dismissed the idea that it mattered that Grace came from poor labouring folk and had been a servant. A humble origin did not prevent her having the grace and gifts necessary to make her a fitting wife. Indeed, he thought it would be harder to find a gentlewoman who possessed the necessary qualities because in his opinion wealth tended to corrupt. Grace was used to living simply and she would desire nothing more than she already possessed. Unlike Charles' wife, she would not involve incurring additional expense to the Methodist movement and he had already cleared it with her that, if they had children, she would be willing to have them 'wholly brought up at Kingswood' so that they would not distract him from his work. He accepted that

247 17 Nov 1742 letter to Mrs Martha Hall in A. Clarke, Memoirs of the Wesley Family, London 1860 Vol II pg 337-8
248 H. Rack, Reasonable Enthusiast, Epworth (third edition) 2002 pg 263

Charles was probably right in saying that some would attempt to blacken her character because she had been his servant, but he saw no reason to surrender to such slander – it was no more hurtful than many other insults that he and she had faced. The truth was that, because she had been his servant, he had got to know her in ways that would have been otherwise impossible. As to the question of impropriety over her having travelled with him, he thought that a nonsense – 'let them know withal I shall never marry any woman till I had proof that she could and would travel with me'.[249]

The key question for John was not her social status but whether she was or was not a suitable choice in terms of her behaviour. To answer that he wrote out all the things he admired about her, beginning with her qualities as a housekeeper. First, he comments on her manner of dressing, saying she was 'remarkably neat in person, in clothes, in all things'.[250] This mattered to him:

'A preacher's wife should be a pattern of cleanliness in her person, clothes, and habitation. Let nothing slatternly be seen about her; no rags, no dirt, no litter'.[251]

Grace, in Wesley's words, was 'nicely frugal, yet not sordid':

'She has much common sense, contrives everything for the best, makes everything go as far as it can go, foresees what is wanting and provides it in time; does all things quick and yet without hurry… [She] observes my rules when I am absent as well as when I am present, and takes care that those about her observe them.'[252]

---

249 JWLL pg 77

250 JWLL pg 70

251 Minutes of Several Conversations between Mr Wesley and Others in Works (1872 edition) Vol VIII pg 332-3

252 ibid

Her role as a nurse was exemplary:

'As a nurse (which my poor, shattered, enfeebled carcase now frequently stands in need of) she is careful to the last degree, indefatigably patient, and inexpressibly tender. She is quick, cleanly, skilful, and understands my constitution better than most physicians.'[253]

She had the qualities to be both his companion and friend:

'As a companion she has good sense, and some knowledge both of books and men. She is of an engaging behaviour, and of a mild, sprightly, cheerful, and yet serious temper. As a friend she has been long tried and found faithful. She watches over me both in body and soul, understanding my weaknesses, sympathising with me and helpful to me in all. Never ashamed, never afraid, having a continual presence of mind in all difficulties and dangers, in all enabled to cover my head and strengthen my hands in God.'[254]

The most important question from his perspective was whether she would become 'a fellow labourer in the gospel' and all that he had seen of her told him that she had the 'grace and gifts and fruit' beyond anyone else he knew to fulfil that function:

'She is crucified to the world, desiring nothing but God, dead to the desires of the flesh, the desire of the eye, the pride of life, exemplarily chaste, modest, temperate, yet without affectation. She is teachable and reprovable, gentle and longsuffering,

253 JWLL pg 70-1
254 JWLL pg 71

eminently compassionate, weeping with those who weep, bearing both my burdens, those of the preachers, and those of the people, zealous of good works, longing to spend and be spent for the glory of God and the good of men.

As to gifts, she has a clear apprehension and a deep knowledge of the things of God, a quick discernment of spirits, and no small insight into the devices of Satan. She has been trained up more especially for these ten years in the word of truth..... She is well acquainted with and exercised in our method of leading souls, having gone through all our little offices, and discharged them all entirely well. She has a steady utterance, a spirit of convincing as well as of persuasive speech, a winning address, an agreeable carriage in whatever company she is engaged. By means of all which she is exceedingly beloved almost wherever she comes and is dear, in an uncommon degree, to great numbers of the people.'[255]

His listing of her virtues has been described as not very romantic and 'rather like an exceptionally warm testimonial to an employee of high standing', but that is unfair.[256] He was not writing a love letter. He was simply stating all the reasons why she would benefit his work and so make the perfect wife, helping him serve God even more effectively. He had to confirm in his own mind that Charles was wrong and that his choice made sense:

'[She] greatly assists and furthers me in my work, enlivening my dull and dead affections, composing and calming my hurried thoughts, sweetening my spirits when I am rough and harsh,

---

255 JWLL pg 71-2

256 M. Edwards, The Reluctant Lover: John Wesley as Suitor, Methodist History Jan 1974 pg 54

and convincing me of what is true or persuading me to what is right when perhaps no other could.' [257]

There was, alongside this, a recognition of his sexual feelings towards her. In assessing the benefits of marrying her he says that he had never been able to avoid having sexual desires and he quotes in Greek the famous quotation from St Paul's first letter to the Corinthians: 'It is better to marry than to burn'. Marriage to Grace would not only end his need to suppress his sexual urges but also stop other women pursuing him or misinterpreting his motives. His conclusion was that Grace would be 'a continual defence (under God) against unholy desires and inordinate affections, which I never did entirely conquer'.[258]

The outcome of this listing of her virtues was a ringing endorsement of her suitability to become his wife:

'I never yet heard or read of a woman so owned by God: so many have been convinced of sin by her private conversation, and so many have received remission of sins in her bands and classes or under her prayers... Now show me the woman in England, Wales, or Ireland, who has already done so much good as Grace Murray. I will say more. Show me in all the English annals, whom God has employed in so high a degree? I might say in all the history of the Church... This is no hyperbole, but plain, demonstrable fact.'[259]

This was his state of mind when the two brothers resumed their discussion the next day. John insisted that his feelings for Grace were no temporary infatuation and reiterated his determination to

257 ibid
258 JWLL pg 74
259 JWLL pg 73

marry her . He gave Charles all his reasons. Then he added that he no longer thought there was any scriptural reason for remaining single so why should he be denied the perfect choice of wife? He also doubtless repeated his view that Bennet had no prior claim on Grace and that any promise she had made to him was null and void. When none of this persuaded Charles, John offered what amounted to an olive branch. He said he was prepared to delay marrying Grace until he had won Bennet's approval because he accepted that the movement would suffer if Bennet were to make a fuss and claim that she had been stolen from him. What was required was time to make Bennet realise that John had the rightful claim. He was sure the other preachers would then accept his marriage to Grace if they were presented with 'a fair state[ment] of the case'.[260] This offer did not satisfy Charles. He doubtless saw the pressure that it would place on both men and he probably judged that Bennet would not relinquish his claim. He also rightly assumed that the delay would merely give time for societies to tear themselves apart over the issue. Therefore he remained adamant that John's marriage to Grace was totally out of the question.

John eventually suggested that, as they could not agree, they should put the whole issue before their friend Vincent Perronet for him to pass judgement on whether John should marry Grace or not. Before doing this, the brothers agreed to meet up on 4 October at Leeds, where they could discuss the matter with John Bennet first. John set off on the afternoon of 26 September to continue undertaking his preaching commitments. He says that over the previous couple of days he had not been well, having suffered from diarrhoea, but, with the debate over, he 'grew better every hour' as he travelled to Keswick. He returned to Hindley Hill to rejoin Grace on the evening of the next day, crossing Penrudock Moor

260 JWLL pg 78

and Alston Moor. His description of the journey there talks of him losing his way in a thick mist so he could not see which way to go and then the fog clearing so he thought 'danger was past', but then he says it descended again and he quickly lost his way. It has been suggested that this is as much a description of his psychological state as the physical journey, but there is no reason why at this stage John should have felt any concern. As far as he was aware, the outcome was in God's hands and he felt sure Perronet would calm Charles down. The reason for alarm only occurred when he reached the place where Grace had been staying. This was the house of James and Hannah Broadwood in Hindley Hill. Hannah greeted John with the sad news that Charles Wesley and William Shent had spent a day with Grace and persuaded her to leave with them for Newcastle just two hours before.

John's initial response was to see in this the hand of God and he said: 'The Lord gave and the Lord hath taken away. Bless the name of the Lord.' But, after reflection, he decided he ought to go after Grace. He then changed his mind when James Broadwood offered to pursue them and bring them back: 'In a quarter of an hour, he took horse and I calmly committed the cause to God!'[261] It was a big mistake, not least because Charles Wesley and William Shent were not headed for Newcastle but for Durham with a view to then moving on to Leeds. Broadwood therefore did not catch up with them. It is unclear whether Charles had deliberately misled the Broadwoods on his itinerary or whether this change of route was a subsequent decision, made after he had set off, either because Charles feared that his brother might follow in pursuit or because he felt Grace was liable to change her mind and so speed was of the essence. The sooner she was with Bennet in Leeds the better.

Because Charles's version of events has not survived we are

261 JWLL pg 81

dependent on John's account to know what was said to make Grace leave Hindley Hill. It may or may not be reliable, but the fact he quotes an entire letter from Charles indicates it is likely to be accurate. According to him, Charles arrived at the home of the Broadwoods, kissed Grace's hand, and said: 'Grace Murray, you have broke my heart'.[262] He then promptly collapsed. Whether this was genuine exhaustion or a contrived attempt to win her sympathy, it placed Grace at a disadvantage, as John recognised: 'It is easy to see what impression this must have made on so tender a mind as hers.' When Charles recovered he gave her a letter to read in which he conveyed his feelings. It began by alleging she was acting dishonourably in rejecting Bennet and that this would destroy everything that the revival had achieved:

'My dear sister friend, what shall I say to you? I would not willingly grieve you, though you have well nigh broke my heart and still will be the occasion of bringing down my hairs with sorrow to the grave. Neither my soul nor my body will ever recover the wound in this life.... Fain would I hope that you can say something in your defence..... but the case appears to me you promised John Bennet to marry him – since which you have engaged yourself to another. How is this possible? And who is this other? One of such importance that his doing so dishonest an action would destroy both himself and me and the whole work of God.'

Then Charles cleverly implied that God had helped John to recognise the danger and that therefore John was not going to marry her:

'[The revival] was on the very brink of ruin, but the snare is broken and we are delivered. I am returning with my brother straight to London.... O how humbled, how thankful ought you to be at your almost miraculous deliverance! Had the Lord not restrained you what a scandal had you brought upon the gospel, nay, and you would have left your name as a curse upon God's people.'

It ended by encouraging her to look to Charles for guidance:

'I spare you and hope in ignorance you did it.... I never intend to speak a hard word to you about it, but pray for you and love you.'[263]

The letter worked beautifully because, in John's words, she thought it 'contained my judgement as well as his'.[264] Charles either intended that or was happy to go along with Grace's misconstruction. She, of course, had every reason to trust Charles. She had known him almost as long as she had known John and it was Charles who had acted as her spiritual mentor when she had first joined the Methodists. She had also worked with him at Newcastle and seen how instrumental he was in creating the religious revival. The outcome was that Grace agreed to accompany Charles and honour her promise to marry Bennet. Augustin Leger, who transcribed Wesley's account, comments that 'the mainspring of her ultimate renouncement' lay in the idea that she was not only preserving from ruin 'the work of God' and the reputation of the man she loved but also that 'she thought she was complying with John's wishes'.[265] That ties in totally with Wesley's own comment: 'She believed that it was all by my own

263 JWLL pg 90-2
264 JWLL pg 92
265 JWLL pg 184-5

appointment'.[266]

James Broadwood did not catch up with Charles and Grace because of their change of route. Nevertheless, the journey was not straightforward for Charles Wesley and William Shent because they lost their way. They ended up finding accommodation in Newlands, a township just south of Prudhoe and about twelve miles south-east of Hexham. John says that Grace spent the night 'tumbling and tossing to and fro as one in deep distress'. She wanted to continue believing what Charles had told her and that God wanted her to marry Bennet but her love for John was 'piercing her heart'.[267] The next morning they set off for Yorkshire and rode to Ferry Hill, six miles south of Durham. There they met up with George Whitefield, who told them Bennet was not in Leeds but in Newcastle. Charles, keen to have his friend's support in dealing with Bennet, asked Whitefield to accompany him and Grace back north.

If John Wesley had gone to Newcastle he would have therefore been able to deal directly with first Bennet and then his brother. However, even after James Broadwood returned without Grace, John chose not to go after her. Instead he headed back, on 29 September, towards Whitehaven, determined to give priority to the work of God. This seems bizarre because he must have known that Grace would find it difficult to counter the arguments of Charles, especially as she had long regarded him as her spiritual guide. The explanation appears to lie in the fact that John thought he needed to show that, whatever his love for Grace, his preaching still took priority. He says that his feelings on her disappearance had shown him once and for all just how inordinately in love he was with her. This posed him with a dilemma:

266 JWLL pg 92
267 JWLL pg 94

'Inordinate affection leads from God...[and] makes us less desirous of doing the works of God, less zealous to pray, preach, or do good'. [268]

So far his love for Grace had served only to strengthen his work and make him even more aware of God's presence. It had not even made him jealous of Bennet. Was he now for the first time to put her first? The answer was a 'no'. It had been his custom to tell preachers that they should not travel a mile less or preach one sermon less because they were married. How could he disobey his own command to put God's service before human love? He therefore returned to his itinerant preaching on 29 September and he left what happened to Grace in God's hands:

'I was calm, though sad, looking for help from Him only, to whom all things are possible... If I had had more regard for her I loved than for the work of God, I should now have gone on straight to Newcastle and not back to Whitehaven.'[269]

The one thing that John was absolutely sure about was that God wanted more than anything else 'a full and absolute dedication of your soul and body to him' and it was vital to take the view 'the Lord gave and the Lord has taken away, and wise are all his ways'.[270]

This belief explains the callousness with which John sometimes responded to those occasions when a person lost a partner or even a child, but it did not mean that he was unconcerned about leaving Grace to deal alone with his brother and Bennet. His description of the ride to Whitehaven is of a stormy journey:

268 JWLL pg 82

269 ibid

270 These words come from the advice he gave to a recently widowed preacher. Cited by Leger in JWLL pg 274

'The storm was full in my face and exceeding high, so that I had much difficulty to sit my horse, particularly as I was riding over the broad, bare backs of those enormous mountains. However, I kept on as I could... So thick a fog then fell that I was soon out of all road, and knew not which way to turn.'[271]

There was an equally internal storm in his mind. By the time he reached his destination on Sunday 1 October his heart felt like a sinking stone. He tried to take comfort in the lessons read out in church. They were about Daniel staying true to God in the lions' den and Jesus stilling the storm. Both seemed apt to his circumstances. Was he not showing that he was prepared to sacrifice everything for the sake of his God-given mission and did he not require God's aid to still his aching heart? That evening he opened his Book of Common Prayer and the text his eye fell on seemed equally fitting: 'Deliver me not over unto the will of my adversaries'. He hoped God would strengthen Grace and prevent her surrendering to the wishes of his brother and Bennet. The historian Henry Rack has aptly written:

'He really wanted a voice from God; or perhaps one should say that he hoped that events would decide the issue and this could be taken as divine guidance.'

That night Wesley had a dream:

'I dreamed I saw a man bring out G.M. who told her she was condemned to die, and that all things were now in readiness for the execution of her sentence. She spoke not one word, or showed any reluctance, but walked up with him to the place. The sentence was executed without her stirring either hand or

271 JWLL pg 83-4

foot. I looked at her till I saw her face turn black. Then I could not bear it, but went away. But I returned quickly and desired she might be cut down. She was then laid upon a bed. I sat by mourning over her. She came to herself and began to speak, and I awaked.'[272]

There have been a number of attempts to psychoanalyse this. One possible explanation is that it shows he thought Grace had brought on the death of their relationship by not rejecting whatever Charles had told her. If that were the case, he might mourn her loss but he would not be prepared to listen to her explanations. With the benefit of hindsight, John saw the dream's message as being a simple one: God was forewarning him he would have to resign himself to her loss.

While John was dreaming dreams and proving that his first loyalty was to God and not Grace, Charles was seeking to complete the mission that he believed God had given to him. He was doing all he could to persuade Grace Murray and John Bennet to marry.

---

272 JWLL pg 86 Rack quotation is from Reasonable Enthusiast, Epworth 1989 pg 263

Sally Gwynne, wife of Charles Wesley (from oil painting by John Russell in Charles Wesley's house)

7

GRACE'S MARRIAGE

Getting Grace Murray and John Bennet to marry was not a straightforward task. Charles had to deal not only with a reluctant Grace but also with an incensed preacher. Grace's enemies in Newcastle had so blackened her name to Bennet that he was openly saying he wanted nothing more to do with her. Fearing that he might publicly insult her, Charles kept the couple apart while he did his best to try and undo the damage. To free himself for the task he asked Whitefield to undertake all the main preaching in Newcastle. Whitefield willingly agreed and he reported on the success of this in a letter to the Countess of Huntingdon on 1 October:

'As I am a debtor to all, and intend to be the head of no party, I thought it was my duty to comply. I have preached now in their room four times, and this morning I preached to many thousands in a large close. This evening I am to do the same again. The power of God has attended his word, and there seems to be a quickening and stirring among the souls'.

However, he said nothing to her about the Grace Murray issue – perhaps this was at Charles' request. If Charles persuaded Grace and John Bennet to marry, then clearly the Countess did not need to know about John's affair.

Charles made out to Bennet that Grace was an innocent victim and that the entire fault for all her actions lay with his brother. John Wesley wrote in his account of events that Charles 'laid all the blame upon me' saying that '[I had] used my whole art and authority to seduce another man's wife'.[273] This approach achieved its aim because Bennet no longer felt aggrieved towards Grace – only towards John Wesley. He agreed therefore that he would be willing to marry Grace once she had apologised. Unfortunately the impact on John's reputation in Newcastle was not good because Bennet went round publicly saying: 'If John Wesley is not damned, there is no God'[274] and, as a consequence, many society members renounced their allegiance:

> 'All… were set on fire, filled with anger and confusion… [Sister] Proctor would leave the house immediately. [John] Whitford would preach with Mr W. no more… Another dreamer… saw Mr W. in hell-fire. Jane Keith was peremptory [saying]'John W. is a child of the Devil'.[275]

Bennet's change of heart did not in itself end Charles' problem. There was still Grace to deal with. She had become increasingly determined not to go anywhere near Bennet until she had first spoken with John about what she should do. Charles was supposed to be meeting up with John in Leeds on 4 October. This was not a deadline he could meet. He asked Whitefield to head south in his stead, saying he would follow as soon as he had managed to secure the marriage of Grace Murray to John Bennet. Whitefield was not at all sure that Charles was doing the right thing but he did as his friend asked. Once Whitefield had left, Charles, under pressure to resolve the matter as quickly as possible, stooped to base deceit. He told Grace that John had no intention of ever seeing her again unless she sought Bennet's forgiveness for not honouring her commitment

273 JWLL pg 94
274 JWLL pg 95
275 ibid

to marry him. A weeping Grace was dragged before Bennet. She fell at his feet, acknowledged she had used him ill, and begged his forgiveness. Then, according to the account written later by John, Charles cruelly deceived her so she would be willing to be 'sacrificed' to Bennet:

> One was brought in to assure her, 'I had given her up and would have nothing more to say to her. Only I had ordered him to procure some place among the country societies where she might live privately'. Upon this, one cried out, 'Good God! What will the world say? He is tired of her, and so thrusts out his wh[ore] into a corner. Sister M. will you consent to this?' She answered, 'No, I will die first'. So, seeing no other way, she frankly declared 'I will have John Bennet if he will have me'.[276]

On 3 October John Bennet and Grace Murray were married at St Andrew's Church in Newcastle by its curate, Andrew Brewster, with Charles signing the register. Some of those who are most critical of Charles' behaviour allege his fears about the impact of John marrying Grace were needless:

> 'It is true that for a time the societies would have been divided in their view of the marriage, but as Grace's qualities revealed themselves, criticism would have quickly died and she would have been accepted as his true helpmeet'.[277]

However, although that is a possibility, a stronger case can be made to support Charles' view of the matter. There is no doubt that many societies would have turned their back on John's leadership

276 JWLL pg 95-6
277 M.Edwards, The Reluctant Lover: John Wesley as Suitor, Methodist History Jan 1974 pg 57

if Charles had permitted him to marry Grace. They would have accused John not only of hypocrisy (because he had long vowed to remain celibate and encouraged others to do so) but also of riding roughshod over the rights of others (because he was pulling rank and marrying a preacher's intended bride). Grace's status as John's servant made public dissension even more likely. Two-thirds of the membership was female and many women would have gossiped endlessly about what Grace had or had not done as John's servant on their travels together in order to seduce him. How could John's moral authority have survived this? When Charles subsequently defended his actions he said he had saved the religious revival from imploding and he was probably right. In the words of the nineteenth century historian Luke Tyerman: 'His alarm was reasonable and his interposition needed'.[278]

Yet it is still difficult to justify Charles' behaviour. In his determination to prevent the marriage, he resorted to lies and deceit and he undoubtedly pressurised Grace into marrying Bennet. Understandably therefore most historians have strongly criticised him:

'He had no right absolutely to judge and determine for his brother in a matter so sacred. Counsel and remonstrance he might have given, and that with all the earnestness of which he was capable; but beyond this he was not justly authorised to proceed.'[279]

More recently it has become fashionable to say that his behaviour was so hysterical that he must also have been driven by personal motives. It has been suggested that Charles's opposition sprang from

---

278 L. Tyerman, Life and Times of JW, London 1871 Vol II pg 55
279 Thomas Jackson, Life of C.W, John Mason, London 1841 Vol 1 pg 540

jealousy and possessiveness and that he feared he might lose his special relationship with his brother if John got married. However, this ignores the fact that Charles himself had acquired a new special relationship – with his wife, Sally. As indicated earlier, it has also been suggested that Charles feared John would provide less money for him and Sally to live on if he got married, not least because John would lose the money from his Oxford fellowship, which was conditional on him staying single. This argument carries no weight from a financial perspective because the money coming from Methodist publications was sufficient to meet the needs of both brothers. However, it is fair to say that John already disapproved of providing the size of income that the Gwynnes had demanded for their daughter and marriage to the much less demanding Grace would have amplified his discontent. Nevertheless, it is hard to see Charles being motivated by sordid financial considerations, given his love for his brother and his normal generosity of spirit.

Although it may seem odd, Charles' hardness of heart on his brother's affair probably stemmed from how well he knew John. It was from the best and not the worst of intentions that Charles behaved so appallingly. He knew that his poor health would not enable him to undertake more should John decide to do less, and there was no obvious replacement leader. The future of the revival therefore required John to remain single. In this context it is worth quoting the words of the nineteenth-century editor of Charles' journal, Thomas Jackson:

'The fact is, Charles regarded his brother as providentially called to superintend that extensive revival of religion which had now, for several years, been carried on by their joint labours and that of their fellow-helpers. To reserve the work in unimpaired efficiency and extend it according to their hopes he knew would require his brother constantly to itinerate through Great Britain and Ireland; and such incessant journeying was incompatible with the comfort of a married life.'[280]

This was not too much to demand of John because Charles was absolutely convinced not only that John's feelings for Grace were no more than a temporary infatuation but that his brother was intrinsically unsuited for matrimony. He had good reason to think so. He had seen John flirt with a number of women over the years and he knew from personal experience that his brother had no understanding of what made for a happy and successful marriage. Domestic pleasures were simply not on John's agenda, however much he might think they were. He hated any time that was not spent on evangelism and service. Many years earlier John had helped Charles avoid a potentially disastrous marriage with a pretty but unsuitable actress called Molly Buchanan and Charles probably thought he was now reciprocating in preventing John making a similar disastrous decision. He probably also thought he was acting in Grace's best interests because he assumed that she would be far happier married to John Bennet than she ever would be to his brother. This judgement may well have been a correct one. Bennet was far more of a family man than John Wesley and Grace was to have a very happy marriage with him.

On the evening of 4 October John Wesley arrived in Leeds and met up with George Whitefield at the shop belonging to William Shent in Briggate.[281] Whitefield waited until they were alone together before telling him that Charles was not yet in Leeds because he had remained in Newcastle in order to persuade John Bennet and Grace Murray to marry. The news plunged John into dismay:

---

280 ibid pg 539

281 This was not unexpected because he had received a letter on 2 October in Whitehaven from Whitefield saying that they should meet when he got to Leeds.

'I was troubled. He perceived it. He wept and prayed over me. But I could not shed a tear. He said all that was in his power to comfort me, but it was in vain. He told me, 'It was his judgement she was my wife and that he had said so to John Bennet, that he would fain have persuaded them to wait and not to marry till they had seen me, but that my brother's impetuosity prevailed and bore down all before it.'[282]

John was understandably confused. Why was Grace, after all her professions of love, listening to Charles? Why was she contemplating turning her back on their 'spousal de praesenti'? Had he done something to offend her? Or was God now determining the issue? And, if so, what had he done that God should punish him in this fashion? He later wrote:

'I felt no murmuring thought [against her], but deep distress. I accepted the just punishment of my manifold unfaithfulness and unfruitfulness, and therefore could not complain. But I felt the loss both to me and the people, which I did not expect could be repaired. I tried to sleep but I tried in vain for sleep was fled from my eyes. I was in a burning fever, and more and more thoughts still crowding in my mind, I perceived, if this continued long, it would affect my senses. But God took that matter into his hand, giving me on a sudden sound and quiet sleep.'[283]

It has been suggested that Wesley's final sentence indicates he dealt with his inner conflict by an act of dissociation (i.e. that what had happened was nothing to do with him but the hand of God at work).

282 JWLL pg 87
283 ibid.

Certainly he tried to believe that, if he did not succeed in marrying Grace, then it would be because God had a reason for denying him marriage to Grace:

> 'Unsearchable thy judgements are,
> O Lord, a bottomless abyss!
> Yet sure thy love, thy guardian care,
> O'er all thy works extended is.
> O why didst thou the blessing send?
> O why thus snatch away my friend?
>
> What thou hast done I know not now!
> Suffice I shall hereafter know!
> Beneath thy chast'ning hand I bow:
> That still I live to Thee I owe.
> O teach thy deeply-humbled son
> To say, 'Father, thy will be done!'[284]

Remarkably Wesley did not head off the next morning for Newcastle to intervene in what was happening. Instead he accompanied Whitefield, who preached in the morning in Leeds and in the late afternoon in Birstall, where John Nelson joined them. It was on their return to Leeds that a messenger arrived at about eight o'clock carrying the news of the marriage. An hour later Charles arrived. Understandably John was reluctant to meet him, but Whitefield and Nelson, keen to act as arbiters, got him to change his mind. The four men met together. Far from being apologetic, Charles took the moral high ground, arguing that he had only been forced to take the action he had because of his brother's sinful behaviour in brushing aside Bennet's prior claim to marry Grace. He said he ought by

284 JW's Poem on Grace Murray

rights to have no more conversation with John than he would with 'an heathen man or a publican'. John says that this accusation had no impact on him: 'I felt little emotion. It was only adding a drop of water to a drowning man.'[285] Whitefield and Nelson burst into tears, praying that the brothers would be reconciled.

John, of course, at this stage still had no clue as to what Charles had done to persuade Grace to marry Bennet. He simply assumed that Grace had deserted him and he believed she had chosen to put the blame for their love affair on him – hence Charles' indignation. Whitefield and Nelson prayed and entreated the brothers to remain united. John says he and Charles 'could not speak, but only fell on each other's neck.'[286] It was as this was happening that John Bennet arrived at Shent's house. He and John said nothing but they kissed each other and both of them wept. It was then agreed to let John and Charles speak in private. According to John, he used this time to present his side of the case about his relationship with Grace. As a consequence he says Charles 'clearly saw I was not what he had thought and now blamed her only'. [287]

The next morning John preached at five and both he and Charles then spent time with several of the local preachers. John preached again twice in the afternoon. John says he was then surprised to receive a note saying that the newly married couple wanted to see him. He had assumed from what Charles had said that Grace had no desire to meet him ever again. Their subsequent meeting probably took place in the chambers of a prominent society member called Towers. At first the three of them just wept but then John asked Grace what she had told Charles to make his brother believe he had behaved so badly. Her response and that of Bennet took him by surprise:

285 JWLL pg 88
286 ibid
287 ibid

'She fell at my feet, said: 'She never had spoke, nor could speak against me', uttering many other words to the same effect in the midst of numberless sighs and tears. Before she rose, he fell on his knees too, and asked my pardon for what he had spoken of me. Between them both, I knew not what to say or do.'[288]

It was the first intimation that Wesley had that there was more to what had happened in Newcastle than he had first thought. After dinner, John managed to speak with Grace alone. This immediately threw a totally new light on what had happened. To his horror he discovered that she had never ceased loving him and that her marriage to Bennet had taken place only because of Charles' deceit. Grace had not abandoned him because of failings on his part. Nor had she castigated his character to Charles. Instead she had been led to believe that he had deserted her 'among a thousand other things'. At the same time Charles had led Bennet to think that John's behaviour had been outrageously sinful.

Once John appreciated that Grace and Bennet were victims of his brother's lies, his whole attitude changed. Charles had not just encouraged the couple to marry, he had deliberately misled both of them into taking that step. The enormity of Charles' betrayal hit him hard: 'If these things are so, hardly has such a case been seen from the beginning of the world!'[289] On 7 October he wrote of his feelings to Thomas Bigg, one of his friends in Newcastle:

'Since I was six years old, I never met with such a severe trial as for some days past. For ten years God has been preparing a fellow-labourer for me by a wonderful train of providences. Last year I was convinced of it; therefore, I delayed not, but, as I

288 JWLL pg 96-7
289 JWLL pg 98

thought, made all sure beyond a danger of disappointment. But we were soon afterwards torn asunder by a whirlwind. In a few months the storm was over: I then used more precaution than before, and fondly told myself that the day of evil would return no more. But it soon returned. The waves arose again since I came out of London. I fasted and prayed, and strove all I could; but the sons of Zeruiah were too hard for me. The whole world fought against me; but, above all, my own familiar friend. Then was the word fulfilled, 'Son of man, behold! I take from thee the desire of thine eyes at a stroke; yet shalt thou not lament, neither shall thy tears run down.'[290]

This is an interesting letter because John equates the loss of Grace to the trial he faced when as a child he was caught in the Epworth fire. The reference to making sure that he was beyond danger of disappointment is presumably a reference to his initial statement to Grace that, if he were to marry, it would be to her. This was hardly the decisive move that he makes it out to be. The reference to being torn apart by a whirlwind must refer to the subsequent claim from Bennet that he had a prior claim on Grace and her agreement to marry him. However, the fact John took her to Ireland did not mean the storm had blown over and his actions in dealing with Bennet's continued claim can hardly be described as John striving to do all he could. John might have thought he had handled his growing love for Grace well, but that was not the case. John's conclusion was that 'the whole world' had fought against his desire to marry Grace, but that the really decisive action had stemmed from Charles, 'my own familiar friend'.

---

290 Letter is reprinted in JW Works (1872 edition) Vol XIII pg 162-3. In the Bible the sons of Zeruiah were the nephews of King David and brave soldiers in the royal army. Although they were among his closest companions and very committed to serving David, they sometimes chose to act against his express wishes.

There seems to have been no immediate exchange between the brothers because their different preaching commitments kept them apart. That explains why, on 8 October, Charles sent a letter to a friend in London about how well the work of the revival was going, especially now that they were working with Whitefield again: 'GW and my br[other] and I are one; a three fold cord which shall no more be broken'. [291] John travelled up to Newcastle on 9 October. During that journey he poured out his feeling in a thirty-one verse poem. Its first lines read:

> 'O Lord I bow my sinful head!
> Righteous are all thy ways with man!
> Yet suffer me with thee to plead,
> With lowly reverence to complain,
> With deep, unutter'd grief to groan,
> O what is this that Thou hast done!'[292]

All he could do was pray that in future God would be his only love:

> 'Teach me, from every pleasing snare
> To keep the issues of my heart
> Be thou my love, my joy, my fear!
> Thou my eternal portion art.
> Be thou my never-failing friend,
> And love, O love me to the End!'[293]

When he got to Newcastle, doubtless he heard more about what had happened. He seems to have judged at this stage that Bennet was not

291 To Ebenezer Blackwell. Letter is postmarked from Sheffield on 11 Oct but its contents indicate it was written probably three days before that. DDCW 1/24 John Rylands Library

292 Wesley's Lost Love

293 ibid. This is the poem's last verse.

to blame for what had happened. He wrote to Bennet on 10 October in a conciliatory tone, calling him his 'dear brother' and expressing the hope that they could return to the kind of relationship they had once enjoyed:

'O let every warm or unguarded word which either of us has expressed either in speaking or writing (too, too many such I charge myself with) be forgotten from this moment'.

He asked for forgiveness and urged that the two of them 'now go hand in hand, pressing to the mark, the prize of our high calling in Christ Jesus'.[294] The only hint in the letter of any potential for disagreement is a reference to Bennet's inclination to accept Calvinist theology. Wesley warns him against being influenced by Whitefield, saying it would hinder his usefulness among the societies.

When John returned to Leeds on 17 October, he agreed to preach alongside Bennet. In his journal Wesley recounts going the next day with the lay preacher to Rochdale and Bolton. Whether Grace was with them or kept out of John's sight is not clear. In Bolton they faced an attack from a dangerous mob. Over the next couple of days Wesley went to various places before heading southwards towards first Wednesbury, and then Dudley and Birmingham, which he reached on 24 October. He continued preaching as he travelled on, reaching Kingswood on Saturday 28 October. Charles went to greet him but not without some trepidation. He confided in a secret passage in his journal the outcome:

'No love or joy or comfort in the meeting. No confidence on either side. He did not want to talk to me.'[295]

---

294 MS Letter Book of John Bennet pg 75 John Rylands Library
295 The Manuscript Journal of Rev CW, Kingswood Books 2007 Vol II pg 583.

It was immediately apparent to Charles that John's feelings for Grace were not the short-lived infatuation that he had presumed and that his brother was yearning still to marry her. At their meeting John told Charles in no uncertain terms that there was no excuse for what he had done and Charles, in his anguish, wrote in a subsequent letter to their mutual friend, Vincent Perronet:

'[He was] insensible both of his own folly and danger, and of the divine goodness in so miraculously saving him'. [296]

On the Sunday Charles travelled back to Kingswood so he could assist his brother offer Holy Communion, but, behind the public front, was a gaping chasm. By this time Charles had heard from John's travelling companion, David Trathern, that not only had his brother spent time in private with Grace Murray but that he was still 'desirous to marry':

'Dead, dead, dead at the Sacrament. Rode back quite miserable… Mournful discourse with Sally. Lost all strength and heart; weighed down to the earth.' [297]

Charles told Perronet of the bitter argument that he and John had that evening:

'Forced by his impatience, I had showed him my account of what lately has happened… It had the effect I expected. He denied the whole. William Shent's account was all lies. Jane Keith's was all lies. His only was all true. He had been in no fault at all, in no passion or inordinate affection, but had done

296 30 Oct 1749 DDCW 10/2 John Rylands Library
297 CWJ Oct 29 1749. Secret passage in Manuscript Journal of Rev. CW, Vol II pg 583

all things well and with the utmost calmness and deliberation. He had been in no temptation; the church and work in no danger. That was nothing but my needless panic. As soon as I could recover my astonishment I told him plainly he was given up to Jewish blindness of heart… I declared I would cover his nakedness as long as I could, and honour him before the people; and if I must at last break with him, would retreat gradually, and hide it from the world. He seemed pleased with the thought of parting, though God knows, as I told him, that I had saved him from a thousand false steps and still I am persuaded we shall stand or fall together…What the end of this thing will be only God knows, but the cloud at present hanging over us looks very black.'[298]

This is not the only occasion when Charles makes reference to having written an account of his role in preventing John's marriage to Grace, but sadly it has not survived. It is obvious he felt his actions had been justified, but he did not want what had happened to destroy his relationship with his brother, whose agony was far greater than he had expected. Charles says that his own soul was so 'exceeding sorrowful' that he became physically ill and he had to abandon his preaching commitments. John continued to preach publicly, but Charles comments that, when he heard him on 2 November, he was very unlike himself. It must have been very hard for John. Not only had he lost Grace, but also his brother appeared to him unrepentant. Moreover, he had to witness how happily Charles was married – a marriage that he had helped facilitate, even though he had disapproved of his brother's choice of partner. Charles should have been more empathetic towards John's distress, even if he did believe his actions were necessary.

298 30 Oct 1749 DDCW 10/2 John Rylands Library

John's distress spilled over in a letter that he sent to Bennet on 3 November. This was very different in tone from the one written on 10 October. He said he had loved Bennet 'before and since' the marriage, but the preacher had done him 'the deepest wrong which I can receive on this side of the grave':

'I was never yet convinced that your [marriage] was according to the will of God… [or] consistent either with justice, mercy or truth… They who know the whole affair know that I have been the greatest sufferer, but not the greatest sinner. Not that I can clear myself, neither. I loved you both too well.'

The letter shows a very unbalanced mind. In one section John apologises to Bennet for not speaking plainly enough and for not talking through with him the extent of his feelings, and says that the couple had done the right thing in marrying in order to cure him of his faulty behaviour. However, this is then followed by an attack on Bennet:

'I left with you my dearest friend, who was necessary to me as a right hand, as dear as a right eye. One whom I looked upon then (and not on slight grounds) as contracted to myself… One I loved above all on earth, and fully designed for my wife. To this woman you proposed marriage, without either my knowledge or consent. Was this well done?…. You wrote me word you would take no further step without my consent. Nevertheless, not only without my consent, but with a thousand circumstances of aggravation, you tore her from me whether I would or no – when all I desired was to refer the whole to impartial men! And all the blame lies upon me! And you have acted with a clear conscience to this day!'

John even blames Bennet for wrecking the religious revival by destroying his relationship with Charles:

'My brother does not preach at all. Neither hath he spoken with me since Sunday. I claim no obedience from you or any other preacher. On [Wednesday] I shall set out for London. For here I cannot be. I know not whether anything remains for me to do with regard to you but to give you both up to God.' [299]

That same day John tackled his pregnant sister-in-law over what had happened. Charles was aghast when he heard about this, not least because Sally had been unwell for weeks. He once again confided what was happening to Vincent Perronet:

'[He] took my wife into his room… and read her his own account, trying all he could to make a difference between her and me. She could say nothing to his confident assertions, though [he engaged in] the grossest misrepresentations and falsifications of facts. This last act of unkindness wounded me more than all the rest'.

Charles conveyed his gratitude that Perronet's son, Edward, had supported him by making clear to John that he would have been one of those who would have refused to continue serving him had he 'acted so basely' as to marry Grace. [300] It is not clear when but Charles wrote to Bennet urging him on no account to let Grace ever see his brother again.

Despite these scenes, the brothers tried to put on a public face as best they could. On 8 November they set out together, accompanied

299 MS letter book of John Bennet pg 76-7 John Rylands Library
300 4 Nov 1749 DDCW 10/2 John Rylands Library

by Edward Perronet, to go to London. There they undertook their respective duties for a week prior to the commencement of the annual conference on 16 November. This was to prove a disaster. John was too wounded not to use the occasion to try and humiliate Charles.

The Foundery in London (from print in the New Room)

Molly Vazeille, wife of John Wesley (from painting by unknown artist)

8

WESLEY'S REACTION

According to Charles, John showed 'the utmost uneasiness and impatience' at the Methodist Conference and said if he could not have the authority he required without Charles' interference he would rather have none at all. He claimed that Charles was ruining everything and at one point he threatened 'to run away and live beyond [the] sea'. It took all Perronet's skills to humour John 'into tolerable temper'.[301] Even then, John did everything he could to assert his authority over Charles. First, he made clear that henceforth he would expect all the religious societies nationwide to look on the Foundery as 'the mother church'. This was not just about subjugating the New Room in Bristol and the Orphan House in Newcastle, both of which were strongly under Charles' influence, but about asserting his authority over the entire movement. John's sermons and the minutes of conference were to become the handbooks on what Methodism believed and how it should be organised. John knew the phrase 'mother church' would be deeply offensive to his brother because for Charles there was only one mother church and that was the Church of England.

Secondly, John persuaded the Conference to radically increase the number of lay preachers, although he knew both Charles and George Whitefield did not want that. They felt they were just beginning to persuade a small group of clergy to back the revival

301 CWJ 17 Nov 1749. Secret passage included in S.T. Kimbrough & K. Newport, Manuscript Journal of Rev. CW, Kingswood Books 2007 Vol II pg 585

and that creating more lay preachers would simply drive those clergy away. Indeed, from Charles' perspective, creating more lay preachers was a deliberate encouragement to those who believed Methodism should become a separate sect. To add insult to injury, John demanded that Charles should take responsibility for training and monitoring the new preachers. Charles refused to do so.

This conference was the first indicator that the tension created by Charles' prevention of John's marriage was, in the words of one historian, becoming 'hopelessly entangled with bitter debates over the future of Methodism'.[302] Judging from letters written by John and Charles, the conference might also have been the first occasion when the Grace Murray affair was aired in public. Charles told Bennet:

'What provoked our friend [JW] to that rash exposing himself (not me, not you) was my showing my account to some of the preachers. Then the enemy took occasion, and urged him to read his to our stewards and a few more.'[303]

And John wrote:

'Where my brother had spoke, there I spoke – just as much as I believe the glory of God required. And all to whom I spoke said, with one voice, 'You are still as much prejudiced in her favour as ever'.[304]

Charles left London thinking 'there was no good to be done' and he half-resolved never to attend another conference. He returned to Bristol exhausted with 'pain of body and vexation of spirit' and with

302 G. Lloyd, CW and the Struggle for Methodist Identity, OUP 2007 pg 105
303 8 Jan 1750 DDCW 1/94 John Rylands Library
304 9 Feb 1750 MS Letter Book of John Bennet John Rylands Library

little inclination to preach.[305] There he was comforted by his wife and a number of the female society members, including Sarah Perrin, the housekeeper at the New Room. The scale of John's distress and its impact on the way he was handling affairs led George Whitefield to write to the Countess of Huntingdon that November to suggest she intervene to take over the running of the revival because 'a leader is wanting'.[306] For similar reasons Vincent Perronet wrote to Charles, urging him to persevere in seeking a proper reconciliation with John for the sake of the revival:

'Soothe his sorrows. Pour nothing but oil and wine on his wounds. Indulge no views... but what tend to the honour of God... and a healing of our wounded friend. How would the Philistines rejoice, could they hear that Saul and Jonathan were in danger from their own swords!'[307]

Charles' response to Perronet shows how depressed he had become about the huge deterioration in his relationship with John:

'I thank you for speaking with my brother, but... I am no longer of his council... He has brought down my strength and I am next to useless. For when I preach, which is very seldom, my word is without power or life. My spirit is that of the whole people. All are faint and weary. All seem on the brink of desperation.'[308]

One of Charles' big concerns was that, in his anger, John had vowed to prove his brother wrong about his unsuitability for marriage.

---

305 CWJ 1 Dec 1749 ibid pg 585-6

306 J. Gillies, Works of GW, London 1771 Vol II pg 294

307 Quoted in T. Jackson, Life of Rev. CW, Vol I London 1841 pg 540

308 CWJ 13 Dec 1749. Letter copied in secret passage included in S.T. Kimbrough & K. Newport, Manuscript Journal of Rev. CW, Kingswood Books 2007 Vol II pg 586

He was proclaiming that he would shortly marry someone without letting Charles know in advance who it was. Charles told Perronet on this issue he could only hope God would find a way of preventing this happening just as he had used him to stop John marrying Grace:

'His late deliverance by my ministry, and present silence of the world, gives ground to hope God will save him in spite of himself... We do not know what to do, but our eyes are unto you. Arise, O God, and maintain thine own cause.'[309]

John's anger was sufficiently directed against Charles that he decided to apologise to Bennet for the letter that he had sent him. On 7 December he wrote:

'I wrote my last out of the fullness of my heart, not then knowing that I should write to you any more. I do not care to write anything fresh on that subject. Perhaps I may sometime show you the letters I designed for you in time past. I do not see these things in the same light as you do. But I complain not. For I am a sinner. Therefore it is just that I go heavily all my days. Nay, I believe it is best for me. I am your affectionate brother.'

And he added some words specifically for Grace:

'Poor Grace. You have formerly been a means of many blessings to me. May God prepare you to receive all his blessings, in time and in eternity.'[310]

Unaware of this, Charles wrote in January to Bennet, urging him

309 CWJ 23 Dec 1749 ibid pg 586-7
310 Arminian Magazine. Copied out by Gifford Bennet in Feb 1896

not to retaliate if his brother continued to prove difficult. It was incumbent on both of them not to let the revival be destroyed by acrimony:

'Our enemy [the Devil]'s design is to induce him or me to publish that affair by any means so as to stop the course of the gospel and scatter the flock. Let us not be ignorant of his devices. All private resentment must be sacrificed to public good. Our calling is to suffer all things that the gospel be not hindered. For God's sake, and His people's, possess your soul in patience. I have need of patience too... There is a wonderful revival of the work in London. God forbid we should obstruct, much less destroy it. But this would be the sure effect of our vindicating ourselves.'[311]

William Brigg sent a similar word of warning to Bennet from London. Although he was complimentary about the work that John was doing at the Foundery, he was not happy about John's state of mind and he urged Bennet not to say anything at all about what had happened because it would only serve to damage the revival.[312]

It was probably as a way of getting back at Charles that John Wesley commanded Bennet to implement the policy that his brother had opposed at the Conference in November. He instructed him to encourage all religious societies, whatever their origin, to join in the new 'general union', which would have John Wesley as its 'Superintendent'. Bennet's journal that month recounts how he and Grace went to various places, including Bolton, Astbury, Davyhulme, Shackerley, Rochdale, Milner's Barn, and Todmorton. It can be assumed her role was an active one because Bennet refers

311 8 Jan 1750 DDCW 1/94 John Rylands Library
312 16 Jan 1750 MS Letter-Book of John Bennet John Rylands Library

to Grace meeting with the women bands at Milner Barn and how she found them 'simple, teachable, and tender hearted' though 'exceeding weak in the faith'.[313] Even in the midst of undertaking this work Bennet was obviously slightly on edge about whether he could regain John Wesley's trust. At Rochdale, for example, he saw 'something very strange' in the manner of Christopher Hopper and John Brown, who had come down from Newcastle, and he judged they had been sent by Wesley to spy on him. [314]

The preacher William Darney met up with Bennet at Todmarton and he heightened Bennet's concern by saying that Wesley was persecuting him because of his Calvinist views. How, asked Darney, could you work for a man who was so autocratic and who could not bear anyone to disagree with him? How could you trust someone who invited you to join his connection and then kicked you out as soon as you had handed over the societies you had created? Bennet went with Darney to see William Grimshaw at the end of the month, probably to air their worries and concerns. By this stage Bennet was hearing from many quarters that Wesley was seeking to blacken his character among some of the preachers and societies. The meeting proved ill-timed. Grimshaw had sent his son and daughter to be educated at Kingswood School and he had just heard that his daughter Jenny had taken ill and died there. On 29 January Bennet went on to Keighley with Grace. She held a meeting for both the single and married women belonging to its Methodist society while he preached to the men. The couple then moved on to Bradford and Birstall before attending the Methodist Quarterly Meeting at Leeds. This was not without some trepidation on Grace's part because she was worried about how some of the societies were viewing her.

In February Charles Wesley had to cope with the tragedy of his

313 24 Jan 1750 JBD pg 197
314 23 Jan 1750 JBD pg 196

wife Sally having a miscarriage. He attributed this to the impact on her of the division between him and John, and he confided to his friend Vincent Perronet:

'My brother has cast poison into my cup of temporal blessings and destroyed as far as is in him lay all my future usefulness to the Church... Once I had great zeal and strong desires to be used as an instrument in his work; but I now only desire to rest.'[315]

Charles decided to take Sally to her family home in Ludlow to convalesce. Both of them were almost killed whilst attempting to cross the swollen River Severn. Charles interpreted this as a signs of God's disapproval for his inaction in the work of the revival. His friends urged him to promise obedience to John's wishes and so he met up with John in Oxford to try and patch up at least a public display of unity. However much John loathed what Charles had done, he knew he could not afford to totally alienate his brother. Charles' contribution to the revival was far too essential to be lost. As a consequence Charles was able to write to Bennet on 2 March to inform him that the outcome of the meeting was that John was 'quite willing to bury all past matters in oblivion.'[316] This was not to prove true. The complete mutual trust they had once enjoyed was lost forever.

The Bennets finally returned home to Chinley at the beginning of March, probably because Grace's pregnancy was making continued travel impossible. There was no way she could maintain the fortnightly two hundred mile tour of societies that had become her husband's usual routine. The couple found not only Charles' letter but two letters awaiting them from John Wesley, one dated 23

315 9 Feb 1750 DDCW 10/12 John Rylands Library
316 2 March 1750 DDCW 1/33a John Rylands Library

January and the other the 9 February. Both letters showed that there were people out to make mischief. At some stage early in January someone had sent Wesley the transcript of a letter that Bennet had sent to John Haughton, a preacher with whom he had worked and who was then based in Ireland. The letter included the following paragraph:

'I was married to Grace Murray on Tuesday... by the advice of Mr C[harles] W[esley] and G[eorge] W[hitefield]... But when Mr [Wesley] came to hear it, and saw us, he was so enraged as if he had been mad, for he himself was inflamed with love and lust unto her'. [317]

The letter dated 23 January was John Wesley's furious response. It was not just that Bennet was talking about what had happened behind his back but that he was daring to accuse him of being inflamed with lust. Rightly or wrongly, Wesley attributed this description of his behaviour to Grace:

'How came you to know that 'I was inflamed with lust'? Did your wife tell you so? If she did not, you would not have so roundly affirmed it. If she did, she has made me a fair return. If you only, after having robbed me, had stabbed me to the heart, I might have perhaps endeavoured to defend myself. But I can now only cover my face and say, 'Art thou also among them! Art thou, my daughter!' [318]

Wesley thus compared her action to that of Cassius's assassination

317 According to what John wrote to Bennet. In a letter sent to Christopher Hopper on 6 February Wesley stated that he had also been given evidence to show that Bennet had written foolishly to someone in Newcastle. Presumably someone had reported that to him.
318 MS Letter Book of John Bennet pg 81 John Rylands Library

of Julius Caesar.

The 9 February letter contained a diatribe against Bennet's friend, William Darney. John said he was not prepared to have anyone working for him who talked such nonsense both in his preaching and in his hymn writing. The letter warned Bennet against listening to 'talebearers' if he wanted to retain Wesley's confidence:

'From the time I left you I have continually set a watch before my lips… I spoke my heart once and no more… I have been equally wary in all my letters. Even when the copy of your letter was sent me from Limerick, the sharpest word I wrote in answer was, 'John Bennet is not wise'. My brother, beware you do not hurt yourself.' [319]

With it was a short letter addressed to Grace:

'My dear sister, God forbid that I should cease to pray for you as long as I am in the body. This morning my eyes were filled with tears of joy from a hope that my time here may be short. Many times in a day I commend you to God. May his grace supply all your wants.'

What Bennet thought of the letter to his wife is unknown but he was certainly not happy at the contents of the two letters to him. On 6 March he wrote his reply. First of all, he made clear that anything he had written was solely his responsibility. Grace was in no way privy to any comment he was alleged to have made. Anything he had discovered about John's 'weakness and temptations' was entirely due to Providence. He would never have known about them through his wife who was 'so far prejudiced in your favour'. Secondly, he said

319 MS Letter Book of John Bennet pg 81-2 John Rylands Library

that any rumours that were circulating were not because of him but because of the indiscretions of John and Charles:

'I wish you and your brother had been as wary from the beginning both in writing and talking as I have been; there had not been an occasion for so many mouths to have been opened against the truth'.

As evidence of this, he cited that he was in receipt of copies of letters that John Wesley had written to others:

'I cannot at present but think you had a design to blacken my character amongst the people. Hereby you have raised a jealousy in the people that I am a dangerous man, not to be regarded. This will render me useless. I am asked at Manchester, 'What is there betwixt Mr W[esley] and you? Surely something is amiss.''

Bennet then told Wesley to stop blackening his character or he would have to face the consequences:

'I have hitherto been silent, and not once opened my mouth, but if you prosecute your design, I think I shall be necessitated to relate naked facts. My prayer to God is, that I may never be provoked to discover the nakedness of Israel to those whose hearts and ears are open to everything that may make their road broader to destruction. The devil only will reap the advantage of an open controversy... Through the late commotions, I have learned much, being determined to call no man Rabbi '.

Despite this, the letter still made clear that Bennet was willing to serve Wesley well, providing he was permitted to do so:

'My desire and design is still to go on in the ways and works of

God who will certainly bring us through much tribulation to his desired glory.... My prayer to God is that both you and I may forget the things behind and humbly go on to life eternal.[320]

The letter was not of the kind likely to please Wesley and there is no evidence of further correspondence between them for months. It was perhaps fortunate for the religious revival that there was a far greater issue than Bennet's marriage to occupy most people's attention at this time. A series of minor earthquakes shook London in late March 1750. Many thought it was a sign that the world was about to end. Crowds flocked to pray in church. A revitalised Charles took on the main work in London whilst John engaged in extensive itinerant work. However, what is noticeable is that John chose not to go to any of the northern societies and not to send any of his itinerant preachers.

Bennet began to complain that his work was going unsupported. It made him feel as if he had been suspended from his role as a Wesleyan preacher. On 1 May Charles sent him a letter in which he reassured him that it was not his or his brother's intentional design to neglect Bennet's 'part of the vineyard':

'We have but one body a piece, which can be in but one place at a time. Whether you might not have had an exhorter more frequently spared you I cannot say, not being the orderer of their motions: but I believe my brother makes the most of them and disposes of them more wisely than I or you could. The very reason I presume why he leaves your part so much to yourself, is his just opinion of your diligence and fidelity... Be not discouraged. The Lord of the harvest shall in his time send

---

320 MS Letter Book of John Bennet pg 86-7 John Rylands Library. The reference to the nakedness of Israel was Bennet threatening to expose Wesley's true character. The reference to not calling anyone Rabbi was Bennet's way of saying that he regretted looking to Wesley as his spiritual guide and teacher.

you more fellow labourers.'[321]

This letter was written in a very warm manner. Charles expressed not only his but also his wife's good wishes to both Bennet and Grace. The historian Gareth Lloyd has argued that Charle's efforts to maintain his friendship with Bennet may have been counterproductive because the 'cloying intimacy' of his correspondence simply encouraged Bennet to question the sincerity of the Wesleys.[322] It is difficult to assess whether that was the case or not. What is more certain is that Bennet sought reassurances elsewhere. In June he and a heavily pregnant Grace went to see George Whitefield in Manchester. Whitefield had always had a high opinion of Bennet, describing him as 'as honest-headed a man... as any among us'.[323] The couple spent at least five days in his company, hearing both him and William Grimshaw preach to great effect. In the wake of this, Bennet, probably with their encouragement, once more urged the Wesleys to give him their full support. Once again, Charles offered his and Sally's best wishes and their prayers for Grace's safe delivery whilst providing reasons for his and his brother's continued absence from the north:

'My brother's long and dangerous stay in Ireland had confined me to London and Bristol. It may be a month still before he returns. Then perhaps I may begin my journey to the North.'[324]

Charles was still making excuses in August because John chose to go to Cornwall on his return. He told Bennet it was 'the fewness of the labourers' that made it impossible to send preachers to support

321 1 May 1750 DDCW 1/34 John Rylands Library
322 G.Lloyd, CW and the Struggle for Methodist indentity, OUP 2007 pg 106
323 Quoted in F. Baker ,William Grimshaw 1708-63, Epworth Press 1963 p 159
324 26 June 1750 DDCW 1/36 John Rylands Library

his work.[325] On this occasion he also included a letter to Grace, who was due to give birth:

> 'Dear Grace, Fear not... a little more suffering and the end cometh... My partner [Sally] salutes you in the love that never faileth... She would have rejoiced to see you, but the year is too far spent. Let us hear as soon as our Lord has brought you through your present trial. Peace be with you always. Farewell.'[326]

On 22 August Grace gave birth to a son and he was named John after his father. Charles Wesley congratulated the couple and suggested it might perhaps be a good time for Bennet to take a break from his labours and seek ordination.

On 3 September Charles notified Bennet that his brother was finally going to travel back to the North. He strongly urged Bennet to prevent him meeting Grace and to avoid any discussion of what had happened – 'you must pass an act of eternal oblivion on all sides'.[327] The letter is also interesting because it shows that Charles had been receiving reports that Bennet's increased contact with Whitefield was turning him into a Calvinist. He reassured Bennet it would make no difference to him 'whether you think with Luther or with Calvin', but expressed a hope that Whitefield had not brought him over to his opinions. That is not surprising because Charles knew that if Bennet became an overt Calvinist it would generate more strife with his brother.

Charles' concern was justified. For years Bennet had upheld the Wesleyan view that salvation was for all, even though he had worked with many Calvinists. However, his increased contact with George Whitefield had impacted on his theological thinking and weakened

325 10 Aug 1750 DDCW 1/37 John Rylands Library
326 ibid
327 3 Sep 1750 DDCW 1/38 John Rylands Library

his acceptance of this. From a Calvinist perspective, salvation for all wrongly implied that God's will was 'frustratable'. It led men to boast that they had chosen to be saved instead of recognising that a person was saved only if God selected him or her. Bennet's experiences as a preacher led him to think Whitefield must be right. Most men were sunk in depravity and it was only a select few who were rescued from this state by God.

John Wesley did not go to the North that autumn and one cannot help but feel he was avoiding meeting the Bennets. In his anger at such treatment, Bennet turned increasingly against both the Wesleys. This may explain his comment that he stopped keeping his journal at this time because he was 'sorely exercised and laboured under various temptations' which he chose 'to bury since they may be rather an offence to the weak than otherwise'.[328] Bennet did not go to the annual conference in March when it was held in Bristol. This may have been because of the pressure of his preaching commitments but it may also have been a protest at his treatment. His absence produced a letter from both John and Charles. John wrote 'we should all have been glad to see you here' but the bulk of the letter was a justification of why he was deferring a visit north 'a little longer'.[329] Charles' letter urged Bennet not to turn against working for them and he reminded the lay preacher of what it had personally cost him to ensure his marriage to Grace:

'You and your partner must make amends for the loss of my brother, whose love I have small hopes of recovering in this world. But I find my heart knit still closer to you, and am humbly confident that neither life nor death shall be able to separate us... The lessening of your affection towards my brother must not

328 JBD pg 206
329 12 March 1751 Letter is held at Emory University and transcribed in F. Baker, Letters Vol 26, Works of JW, Clarendon Press 1982 pg 452-3

lessen your affection towards God, or his people or his work… I trust your dearest earthly friend [Grace] is quite recovered. When and where shall we get a sight of you? See and talk with you both, we must.'[330]

When John Wesley eventually travelled to Newcastle in the April of 1751 he went via the north-west. By this time his status had changed because he had married a forty-one year old widow called Mary Vazeille. Maybe he felt he could only face the Bennets if he had a wife by his side. Traditionally his marriage to her is still usually portrayed as a knee-jerk reaction to losing Grace, although the historian Henry Rack challenged this view over twenty-five years ago:

'The gap since the Murray affair suggests that it was not the cliché case of romance on the rebound… He needed a companion and nurse and a bulwark against emotional females and scandal.'[331]

'Molly' (as she was more commonly known) had been known to him and Charles Wesley for a number of years, but seeing her as a possible wife arose only when she nursed him following a fall. Many years later he was to write:

'I married because I needed a home in order to recover my health; and I did recover it. But I did not seek happiness thereby, and I did not find it.'[332]

John had, as promised, deliberately not consulted Charles about his choice. The precise date of the actual wedding is not clear

330 15 March 1751 DDCW 1/41 John Rylands Library
331 H. Rack, Reasonable Enthusiast, Epworth 1989 pg 265
332 J. Telford, Letters of JW, Epworth 1931 Vol VIII pg 223

but it was sometime in mid-February.[333] The nineteenth-century historian Luke Tyerman wrote that the marriage was solemnised by Charles Manning, Vicar of Hayes, one of the clergy sympathetic to Methodism and a friend of both the bride and the groom, but no documentation exists to verify this. In its absence some historians have speculated that the marriage may have been no more than another 'spousal de praesenti' agreement, but with Molly, unlike Grace, insisting the arrangement was immediately made public. Her motives in marrying John are a matter of guesswork, but it is usually assumed, perhaps unfairly, that it was because she felt flattered at receiving his attentions, given his national status.[334]

On paper Molly Vazeille looked a sounder choice than Grace because she had independent means and higher social standing and her age precluded the possibility of children who might divert John from his work. She was a very wealthy widow. It has been estimated she had inherited £10,000 from her dead husband, who had been a prosperous merchant.[335] However, all who knew her – and that included Charles – thought she was a seriously bad choice, partly because she was prone to be rather negative and hot-tempered but mainly because she was not the kind of woman who would be able to offer unconditional support for John's itinerant ministry. When he heard the news Charles could not disguise his horror:

'I was thunderstruck... I groaned all the day, and several following ones, under my own and the people's burden. I could eat no pleasant food, nor preach, nor rest, either by night or by

333 'The Gentleman's Magazine' reported the marriage as having taken place on 18 February and 'The London Magazine' on 19 February

334 In later years John Wesley alleged she had assumed he had considerable wealth and was very disappointed when she discovered that was not the case, but this may only reflect his bitterness towards her by that stage.

335 This was invested in three percent consuls and Wesley expressly ensured that he took none of her money. Instead it was secured for Molly and her four children.

day.'[336]

Unfortunately news of Charles' reaction was communicated to Molly (possibly by John) and this did little to endear relationships, even though Charles tried desperately to rectify that by his subsequent treatment of her.

At the outset of the marriage John addressed Molly with reasonable affection:

'You have surely a right to every proof of love I can give, and to all the little help which is mine my power. For you have given me even your own self. O how can we praise God enough for making us helpmeet for each other! I am utterly astonished at his goodness. Let not only our lips but our lives show forth His praise!' [337]

But it was not long before the relationship became acrimonious. Historians have tended to portray the blame for the subsequent failure of the marriage far more on Molly than on Wesley but that ignores the extent to which she initially tried to support John's work by accompanying him first to Cornwall, then to the north and even on to Ireland as Grace had done. Unfortunately she was not suited by age, temperament, or background to sustain an itinerant lifestyle, and nor was she the kind of person who could cope with her husband travelling without her. Others saw that at once and so should Wesley. The sad truth was that John was not in love with her and she soon realised that and felt neglected. It was while Molly was in Ireland that the preacher John Hampson witnessed the complete breakdown which had occurred in their relationship:

336 CWJ 2 Feb 1751
337 27 March 1751 in F.Baker, Letters of JW 1740-55, Clarendon Press 1982 pg 453

'Had he searched the whole kingdom he would scarcely have found a woman more unsuitable to the prospects of a happy marriage. There never was a more preposterous union… I went into a room and found Mrs Wesley foaming with fury. Her husband was on the floor, where she had been trailing him by the hair of his head; and she herself was still holding in her hand venerable locks, which she had plucked up by the roots. I felt as if I could have knocked the soul out of her'. [338]

One is tempted to wonder whether this incident arose because John had made some comparison between what Molly was failing to do and what Grace had done when she was his companion in Ireland. It is also possible of course that this was the time when John's account of his love for Grace fell into Molly's hands.[339] After Ireland Molly ceased any attempt to regularly accompany John and she began openly complaining that hers was a loveless marriage. Charles Wesley wrote in June 1751:

'Found my sister in tears. Professed my love, pity, and desire to help her. Heard her complaints of my brother. Carried her to my house, where, after supper, she resumed the subject, and went away comforted.'[340]

Charles tried to act as a kind of marriage guidance counsellor. He spent time with Grace alone in 'free, affectionate conference' and then with John, before holding a session with both of them. He says on that occasion he was able to generate 'perfect peace' between them, but, as time went on, Molly grew ever angrier.[341] John's

338 John Hampson, Life of Wesley, London 1791 Vol II pg 124 and 127
339 See Epilogue: A Note on Sources
340 CWJ 21 June 1751
341 CWJ 22 June 1751

attempts to reason with her only annoyed her and she found his self-contained personality equally infuriating. Jealous by nature, she increasingly assumed John preferred travelling without her so he could engage in affairs with other women. It says much for her bitterness that several years later she even accused John of having a long-time love affair with Charles' wife. This infuriated Charles but Sally took the allegation more philosophically, saying nobody would believe Molly on this or on any other issue.

A lengthy letter that John wrote to Molly in 1759 encapsulates many of the issues that he found impossible to handle in his marriage. Molly liked to keep a close eye on who came to see John and he hated 'not having the command of my own house'. He loathed the fact that no one could enter or leave without first obtaining her approval. It made him feel like 'a prisoner'. He hated even more the way she searched through his correspondence and showed others his letters and private papers without his leave:

'My house is not my castle. I cannot even call my study, even my bureau, my own. They are liable to be plundered every day.'

He could not stand the way she constantly talked about him behind his back, 'making my faults (real or supposed) the standing topic of your conversation' and 'slandering me, laying to my charge things which you know are false'. He disliked her constant lies and the 'extreme immeasurable bitterness' she showed to anyone who tried to defend him. Nor could he cope with the way she treated servants:

'You do all that in you lies to make their lives a burden to them. You browbeat, harass, rate them like dogs, make them afraid to speak to me. You treat hem with such haughtiness, sternness, sourness, surliness, ill-nature, as never were known in any house of mine... You forget even good breeding, and use such coarse language as befits none but a fishwife'.[342]

They ended up living completely separate lives and John was not even informed of her death in 1781 until some days afterwards. In his last letter to her, dated October 1778, he wrote what has been described as perhaps the most trenchant letter of rebuke ever written by a famous man to his wife:

'You have laid innumerable stumbling blocks in the way of both the wise and unwise. You have… increased the number of rebels, deists, and atheists; and weakened the hands of those that love and fear God. If you were to live a thousand years twice told, you could not undo the mischief which you have done… I bid you Farewell.'[343]

Obviously the full extent of the misery that lay ahead was not apparent when John finally met up with the Bennets in the May of 1751, but enough had already happened to show he was locked in a miserable marriage. Inevitably this must have revived John's belief that he should have been permitted to marry Grace Murray and rekindled his bitterness towards Bennet. Far from creating a better relationship between the two men, the meeting served only to make matters worse. [344]

342 23 Oct 1759 in J. Telford, Letters of JW, Epworth 1931 Vol IV

343 2 Oct 1778 in J. Telford, Letters of JW, Epworth 1931 Vol VI. The comment was made by Malden Edwards in 'My dear Sister', Penwork 1974.

344 There is no reference in the journal to when they met but it would have been in the May when Wesley was in Yorkshire.

Christopher Hopper (from a print at New Room)

William Grimshaw (from print in the New Room based on engraving by J. Thompson in 1821 Methodist Magazine)

9

DISTRUST AND
DISCORD

At the Bristol Conference Wesley had issued each preacher with an inscribed copy of the minutes of the 1749 Conference. These stated what was doctrinally expected of society members. John and Charles were agreed that they could not accept overt Calvinist preaching from anyone. At the meeting in May John Wesley almost certainly delivered Bennet's copy to him. It read:

> 'To John Bennet. So long as you freely consent to and earnestly endeavour to observe the Rules contained herein I shall rejoice to go on with you hand in hand.'

As already indicated, Bennet had long held sympathetic views towards Calvinism but his respect for the Wesleys had kept those in check. Unfortunately John's handling of the Grace Murray situation had undermined that respect and, during John and Charles's long absence, Bennet had been forced to work more with George Whitefield. As a consequence his Calvinist views had considerably deepened. Indeed in April 1751 he had commenced creating a preaching house in Bolton for those who were responding to Whitefield's inspired preaching.

The task of judging whether Bennet's Calvinism was sufficiently kept under wraps to make him still an acceptable preacher fell to Charles Wesley as part of an inspection that he had agreed to undertake on all the preachers across the entire connection. On his tour of the northern societies he took with him his wife, his sister-in-law Becky Gwynne, and Sarah Perrin, the housekeeper from the New Room. He informed Bennet in August that he going to hold a meeting in Leeds on 11 September and he asked him to bring to it as many preachers as possible. He also made clear how much he was looking forward to seeing him: 'Nothing is of such importance as our meeting at this time'.[345] Charles heard Bennet preach on three occasions and the preacher was not naïve. He chose to pass the test with flying colours. Charles was pleased that he could report to his brother that Bennet was as yet making no attempt to promote Calvinist views. On his way southwards he wrote to Bennet:

> 'I bless God for our last friendly meeting and receive it as a token that we shall never be separated... My heart is more committed to you than ever and our dear sister... I see all things working together for [the] good of the Church. Only we want more faith, more prayer, more patience.'[346]

Unfortunately many of the northern preachers, particularly John Nelson, knew that Bennet was being increasingly outspoken about his Calvinist views and they were keen to shut him up. Charles, operating from a distance, could not prevent a growing animosity developing. In the face of mounting hostility Bennet increasingly found gagging his theological beliefs unacceptable. In October he accused both the Wesleys of imposing 'unscriptural things' on him and assuming 'arbitrary power':

> 'Unless everyman is left at liberty to think and let think I cannot

345 11 Aug 1751 DDCW 1/42 John Rylands Library
346 25 Sept 1751 DDCW 6/44 John Rylands Library

in conscience give you the right hand of fellowship... I cannot in conscience be silent any longer. The cause of Christ constrains me to speak.[347]

In that same letter he also more or less accused both brothers of having openly declared war on him behind a faced of continued friendship.

Charles replied on 26 October saying he wanted say 'a few sincere, although soft words' in reply:

'I appeal to your own calmer judgement... I design never to quarrel with John Bennet, though John Bennet does all he can to force me. But I will not be forced. The second blow makes the quarrel and that (with God's help I promise) I will never give. Try again (if you are not weary of ceaseless provocations) and I will still answer you with words of peace and love... Love is not easily provoked. If you loved me as I do you, you could not so hastily think evil of me.'[348]

He added a note to Grace saying that it was not in any man's power to separate him from her husband:

'For my heart shall not be broken off from you, use me as you will... Need I remind you that ye owe each other (under God) to your faithful and affectionate CW.'[349]

Charles' diplomatic efforts were negated in December by legal action taken over the new preaching house that Bennet had helped

347 4 October 1751 Bennet's Letter Book M/A J92-94 John Rylands Library

348 26 Oct 1751 Autograph manuscript in Wesley Family Collection at Drew University transcribed in K. Newport & G. Lloyd, Letters of CW, OUP 2013 pg 311

349 ibid pg 313-4

create in Bolton. William Grimshaw was determined that he and the Wesleys should have control over who preached within it rather than its trustees.[350] With that in mind he encouraged them on 24 December to sign a document giving the power of appointment to him and the Wesleys. Bennet was furious when he heard about this because no trustee had asked his permission. He was fundamentally opposed to the principle that the Wesleys could dictate who should and who should not preach to the societies and he wrongly assumed that it was a move by John Wesley to get rid of him. In fact Wesley had not even known the action was being taken in Bolton. The preacher Thomas Mitchell has left us a vivid account of Bennet's unhappiness and the impact that had:

> 'The poor people were in the utmost confusion, like a flock of frightened sheep. John Bennet, who before loved and reverenced Mr Wesley for his work's sake, since he got into his new [Calvinist] opinions, hated him cordially, and laboured to set all the people against him. He told them in the open congregation that Mr Wesley was a Pope, and that he preached nothing but popery.'[351]

On 30 December Bennet announced to the society at Bolton he was leaving Wesleyan Methodism and said 'many bitter things of Mr Wesley'.[352] 108 of the 127 society members present then agreed to end their connection with the Wesleys. There is no record of what Grace felt about this dramatic turn of events, but it is reasonable to surmise from later events that she did not welcome the split.[353]

350 A lawyer had argued that any involvement by Bennet might make the document legally invalid because of his status as a dissenter.

351 A Short Account of the Life of Mr Thomas Mitchell, Methodist Magazine 1780 pg 322

352 ibid

353 For example, she rejoined a Methodist society after Bennet's death.

According to the preacher John Oliver, Bennet next made a similar public announcement at the society in Stockport, ending with the words 'Now you must take either me or Mr Wesley'.[354] Only one of its members stayed loyal to the Wesleys. Bennet's actions did not just affect societies. Preachers also took sides. In January 1752 Grimshaw wrote to Charles:

'These intestine divisions are dreadful. While union is preserved among us we are impregnable, and the attacks of our enemies help rather to cement than to distract us: but being divided we become an easy prey to the common enemy, and even worry each other.'[355]

Charles pleaded with Bennet to return to them for the sake of Grace as well as the revival:

'O let me beseech you... not to fall out by the way with your old companions and fellow labourers... God knoweth my heart that it never wandered from you in an unkind thought, since God first brought us together at Sheffield: and never did I feel a stronger desire of eternal union with you than I do at this moment. I cannot bear the thought of ever being separated or estranged from you. I cannot forget our first love and labour of love together... With many tears [I] entreat you to stop before it is too late... You know your own infirmity; which is the same with my brother's. You and he are but too ready to believe evil of each other: for which Satan rejoices. You have often listened to calm advice and not despised even my peaceable love. Your dear partner must and shall help, together with God and me. You

354 An Account of Mr John Oliver: Written by Himself, Methodist Magazine 1779 pg 423
355 Letter quoted in F. Baker, William Grimshaw, Epworth 1963 pg 247-8

will break her heart as well as mine by proceeding violently – if I know anything of her. I am sure she is now under the deepest affliction… Were it possible I would immediately come to see you.' [356]

At the end of the month a letter was issued to all the Methodist preachers. It stated:

'It is agreed by us whose names are underwritten:
1. That we will not listen, or willingly inquire after any ill concerning each other.
2. That if we do hear any ill of each other, we will not be forward to believe it.
3. That as soon as possible we will communicate what we hear, by speaking or writing to the person concerned.
4. That till we have done this we will not write or speak a syllable of it to any other person whatsoever.
5. That neither will we mention it after we have done this to any person.
6. That we will not make any exception to any of these rules, unless we think ourselves absolutely obliged in conscience so to do.'

John and Charles and eleven of their preachers, including John Nelson and William Shent, signed it.

Neither this nor Charles' words could overcome Bennet's bitterness at the ill treatment he felt he had received at John Wesley's hands. In February he wrote to William Grimshaw to say that he now saw the theological views of the Wesleys as a 'root of evil' and that he hoped the minister would join him in 'bringing the offenders

356 23 Jan 1752 DDCW 1/43 John Rylands Library

to justice' even if it meant the revival was broken in the process.[357] Perhaps fortunately for the cause of the Wesleys, family matters took over Bennet's attention at this critical juncture. His mother was taken fatally ill. The initial event that triggered this was Ann Bennet choking upon a piece of hare. According to her minister, James Clegg, her struggles to cough up what was stuck broke 'some vessels in her throat'.[358] By the time Bennet heard the news and reached her, she was very weak. He and Grace nursed her for six days before she died. Both of them were impressed by the faith that she showed and Bennet wrote afterwards:

'[She] dropped many sweet words saying, 'Come Lord Jesus wash me with thy blood, and take me with thy wing'. I then asked her: 'Mother, I hope your soul's happy?' She said, 'Ay, whether I live or die'. Looking at her [i.e. Grace] she said 'Do not watch me, God watches me and will guide me'. I said, 'The Lord comfort you'. She said, 'He does comfort me… My pretty Jesus, my loving Jesus, how tenderly does he deal with me! How does he love me, and I love him'.'[359]

In March Grimshaw wrote to a friend about how he had become much less concerned about the impact of Bennet's desertion:

'The differences occasioned of late by Mr Bennet… will not be so harmful to the churches as a while ago I had feared they would be. Let us pray for the unity and peace of Jerusalem'.[360]

357 27 February 1752 MS Letter Book of John Bennet pg 96 John Rylands Library
358 V.S. Doe, Diary of James Clegg 1708-55, Derbyshire Record Society, Matlock Vol III 1978
359 16 March 1752 JBD pg 206-7. Bennet's Calvinist views caused her some distress because he made her worry for a time that she was not one of the elect, but she later became convinced that she was.
360 Letter to Mrs Gallatin quoted in F. Baker, William Grimshaw 1708-63, Epworth Press 1963 pg 248

The reason for this is made clear by a couple of passages in Bennet's journal where he records how a significant number of society members were less inclined to accept him after his separation from the Wesleys. This applied even in places where he had traditionally been well received. At Woodley near Stockport, for example, he found some 'had made themselves very busy in inviting preachers not only without my advice but contrary to it'[361], while at Stockport he found some members were 'uneasy with me, upon account of my withdrawing myself out of Mr Wesley's connection.' When he told them his reasons it did not satisfy them and he says he was forced to advise them to leave his society. [362]

All this did not stop Charles Wesley continuing to urge Bennet to come to Bristol with Grace so they could effect a reconciliation:

'You may still impute my obstinacy of love to guile or some selfish design I have upon you, but never so will I let you go, or cease pursuing you with all the offices of friendship, and all the prevalence of prayer... Whenever your heart is turned back to us... We are ready waiting to receive you with open arms.'[363]

Bennet rejected this offer in such cold terms that it upset Charles. When John Wesley arrived at Manchester on 26 March he heard from all sides that Bennet was 'still speaking all manner of evil' about him and openly preaching Calvinist views, 'making nothing of Christ' by denying justification by faith.[364] Grimshaw negotiated a meeting between him and Bennet. Initially there appears to have been confusion over when and where this would happen with Grimshaw expecting the venue to be Manchester and Wesley Leeds.

361 17 March 1752 JBD pg 209-10
362 18 March 1752 JBD pg 210
363 3 March 1752 DDCW 1/44 John Rylands Library
364 JWJ 26 March 1752

In the end Bennet and Grace went to Manchester, arriving in time to hear Wesley preach on the evening of 31 March. This may well have been the last occasion on which Grace had any contact with Wesley until, as a widow, she went to hear him preach in 1764. It is highly unlikely they had any opportunity to properly speak together because of the presence of Wesley's wife, although the two men had discussions over the next two days. Wesley wrote nothing about these talks in his Journal but Bennet wrote extensively about them in his.

According to Bennet, on 1 April he told Wesley that there was great unhappiness among the members of the society in Bolton that the trustees had given their preaching house over to Wesley's control. They disliked his desire to only sanction preachers who shared his and Charles' theological views. Bennet argued if Wesley wanted to keep control of the preaching house he ought to recompense the society for its loss. Wesley lost his temper, shouting if it were a matter of money he would give 5,000 guineas whenever the trustees wanted it. Bennet writes:

'I saw it would only exasperate him the more to speak any further upon that head, therefore we dropt it entirely, agreeing to meet the trustees after preaching. I then told him I had something on my mind against him, his brother, and some other preacher, but thought it not proper either to speak of them, or have a conference in their absence. He said if the preachers were in his connection I might speak... While we were thus conversing together Mrs Wesley came into the room in a great rage saying there should be no private meetings, nor underhand dealings. She said I had a gall of bitterness and bond of iniquity and that she believed me to be a very bad man.'[365]

365 JBD pg 211

It is tempting to speculate as to why Molly did this. Was it because John Wesley had frequently confided his dislike of Bennet to her? Did it arise because of her knowledge of John's prior attachment to Grace? Was she angry because Grace was in Manchester? Whatever the reason for her attack it brought the meeting to an abrupt end.

When Wesley preached he used the opportunity to attack Calvinist thinking.[366] This upset Bennet, who judged what was said as being detestably 'unscriptural and unsound'.[367] Following this, Wesley met up with the trustees of the Bolton preaching house and agreed to return money to them. Further discussion about the theological differences became heated:

> 'Mr Wesley rose up in a most violent passion calling me a knave and a villain. His wife charged me to get out of the room and be gone.'[368]

Once again their meeting was hastily ended. The next day Wesley preached three times and he used the occasions to again defend his position. He stated that he had never turned people out of his societies simply for disagreeing with his opinions. This was immediately publicly challenged and Bennet sought to embarrass him by producing a letter that Charles Wesley had written to a farmer called John Cross. Cross had let the Methodists use a room in his house at Northwood as a meeting room and in his letter Charles ordered him to cease inviting two of Bennet's friends, David Tratham and John Webb. They were not to be permitted to preach because of their Calvinist views. John Wesley responded by saying he was not responsible for what his brother had written. Bennet says that he decided not to push matters further in public:

366 Bennet wrote four pages in his journal about the content of this sermon, which he totally disliked.
367 JBD pg 213
368 JBD pg 214

'I had many things upon my mind which I had fully purposed to have spoken but was afraid of quarrelling before the face of the congregation, and so turning the lame out of the way. I was going to have declared and have made my appeal to the society that I never forbid any speaking there although they differed widely from me in their sentiments... He then broke out and said I was a liar... The meeting then broke up.'[369]

Wesley summoned Bennet to a private meeting with him and two of his preachers, Jonathan Haime and Thomas Mitchell, and Wesley's wife joined them. The preachers accused Bennet of making personal attacks on Wesley and of plotting to take over control of the Wesleyan societies. Mitchell also implied that Bennet had been making accusations that Wesley had behaved inappropriately in relation to Grace Murray:

'[He] said I had given broad hints as though Mr W[esley] had been guilty of some uncleaness. I said it was false, I never accused Mr John Wesley of any such thing, neither did I ever believe any such thing. I thought it my duty to clear him of this accusation his wife being present lest some uneasiness should be created between them.'[370]

Bennet refused to get embroiled in a debate with Mitchell and the meeting broke up.

The next day Wesley left for Halifax. Bennet tried to elucidate what instructions had been left about whether he and the other Calvinistic Methodist preachers were still permitted to preach in the Wesleyan societies. Haime told him that Wesley was happy to

369 JBD pg 215
370 JBD pg 216

let Bennet preach to his societies providing he did not contradict or oppose Wesley's doctrines, but that invitation did not necessarily extend to all his associates. John Webb for one was banned. On hearing this, Bennet gave up all thought of preaching ever again in any house ruled by Wesley. He headed off back home with Grace, preaching at Shackerley where the couple were 'kindly received' and at Bolton 'to an extraordinary great congregation'.[371] Despite having a young child, Grace continued to accompany Bennet on his preaching tours over the coming weeks, speaking to the women whilst he spoke to the men. Not all the societies were to prove welcoming as the historian S.R. Valentine has pointed out:

> 'Rumours of betrayal and disloyalty permeated the membership of all the Methodist groups. At each society meeting Bennet and his wife would be met by a wall of whispers and criticisms: 'There is the man who has robbed John Wesley'. In each town or village Bennet would meet with his fellow preachers who, having talked with Wesley and having heard his claims of innocence and injury, would be dismissive and cool in their treatment of the Chinley preacher.'[372]

According to the later writing of her son, Grace was very upset by the split:

> 'This was a heavy affliction to my good mother, who had the highest veneration for the character of Mr Wesley, whom she always honoured as her spiritual father; though she thought his conduct, on that occasion, highly reprehensible. She was then also a warm stickler for the doctrines of universal redemption,

---

371 JBD pg 217-8
372 S.R. Valentine , John Bennet and the Origins of Methodism, Scarecrow Press 1997 pg 261

free-will, etc. which were topics of sharp controversy, at that time, between Mr. Wesley and Mr. Whitefield, my father siding with the latter. But, in a little while, she saw reason to embrace what is commonly called the Calvinistic view of gospel doctrines, in which she acquired a very clear and distinguishing judgement, and was more and more established to the last; though she never afterwards was fond of religious controversy, and advised all her Christian friends against it.'[373]

One consequence of Bennet ceasing to work for Wesley was that Grace had to remove Jackey, her son from her previous marriage, from Kingswood School. One of Bennet's friends, Robert Whitton, was sent in May to fetch the boy, who was about to become eleven years old. Charles Wesley was hugely upset at what he felt was an unnecessary division brought about in part by false allegations directed against him by some of Bennet's companions. He wrote to Bennet to say that he could not be held accountable for what his brother was saying or doing and that Bennet should not believe any evil gossip about his own behaviour without at the very least giving him the opportunity to challenge what people were alleging:

'As to the separation, what shall I say? If I had not the power to hinder, I have not the power to heal it. My only satisfaction is that I laboured all I could to prevent it. I am told that you have spoken much evil of me… But I cannot, will not believe it, till I have your own answer if these things are so?.... [To believe what some say of me] is this thy kindness to thy friend? Is this thy justice? Is it doing what you would be done by, or as I have acted towards you? I never have, and trust never shall, believe evil of you on any testimony whatsoever, till I have given you an opportunity of answering yourself... My partner [Sally] joins in sincere love to Grace and you. We should have been very glad to receive you with your honest friend Robert [Whitton]. I am (and cannot help being) your faithful but afflicted friend'.[374]

The couple were understandably worried about how they were going to survive financially without a preacher's salary coming in, especially as Bennet's father was threatening to disown him and Grace was pregnant again. Bennet was very upset that the societies he had served seemed oblivious of his need for an income:

'I looked so long at the uncharitableness of the people that heaviness seized upon my spirits so as to have effect upon my body. I... was tempted to think that I never should be able to maintain my family, but be reduced to want... I was full of thought touching Jacky Murray who was come from Kingswood School how to maintain him, what school to send him to, how to screen him from my father's eye.' [375]

The possible implication of the last sentence is that Bennet had never informed his parents that Grace had a son by her previous marriage.

Despite the pressures on him, Bennet continued to undertake his preaching tours around the religious societies in Cheshire, Lancashire, and Yorkshire, sometimes accompanied by Grace. He probably learned to avoid the places that were most pro-Wesley and his journal, whilst recording some continued clashes, gives the impression that he was pleased by the loyalty that was shown to him. Certain societies, most notably those in Stockport, Woodley, and Bolton, became his strongholds, even though at first they had been

---

374 18 May 1752 DDCW 1/47 John Rylands Library

375 29 May 1752 JBD pg 224

hesitant about his decision to leave the Wesleys. He did not content himself with revisiting societies because he records also going to new places, including Hollingworth and Saddleworth in Lancashire. In June Bennet heard that John Wesley was holding a meeting with William Grimshaw in Manchester and he decided to go and see them. This did not lead to any reconciliation but it proved a less acrimonious encounter than their previous meeting:

> 'Accordingly we met and spoke our minds fully without the least reserve. I delivered my own soul and told Mr Wesley all that I had heard or feared both of him, his brother and other preachers. We differed in our thoughts touching doctrine, as well as practice. And therefore agreed to part in love'.[376]

Three days later Wesley preached in Bolton and made clear that he had known nothing about the transfer of the preaching house under his name. One of those present questioned him as to why he was preventing Bennet from preaching. He denied that there was any ban on Bennet but this response won him few friends. It was known that Wesley was prepared to let him preach only if he said what John wanted him to say.[377]

Occasionally Bennet was upset by a particular attack on his or his wife's integrity. For example, a curate called Milner in Chipping in Lancashire accused Grace of deliberately encouraging her husband to set himself up in opposition to John Wesley. Bennet defended her, saying she had never had any such design. At the end of July he decided to travel down to a meeting that was being held by George Whitefield in Gloucester with a view to formally becoming a preacher for the Calvinistic Methodist Association. At this point

376 11 June 1752 JBD pg 226
377 14 June 1752 JBD 226

Bennet's journal ends and it is not known what happened there. On 24 December Grace gave birth to their second son, William, at their home in Chinley. Her family commitments put pay to her undertaking itinerant work, especially when she and Bennet subsequently had two more sons.

John Wesley's attitude towards letting any Calvinistic Methodist preach in a society under his control hardened and, following the 1753 annual conference, which was held in Leeds in May 1753, Wesley wrote to Whitefield:

'Between forty and fifty of our preachers lately met in Leeds, all of whom, I trust, esteem you in love for your work's sake... Several of them had been grieved at your mentioning among our people (in private conversation, if not in public meeting) some of those opinions which we do not believe to be true... They conceived... this tended to create not peace, but confusion. They were likewise concerned at your sometimes speaking lightly of the discipline received among us, of societies, classes, bands, of our rules in general, of some in particular. This they apprehended to be neither kind nor just... Above all they had been troubled at the manner wherein your preachers... had very frequently spoken of my brother and me part[icular]ly in the most soffing and contemptuous manner, relating a hundred shocking stories... Two or three... Afterwards desired me in private to mention further that when you were in the north your conversation was not so useful as was expected... [and] that your whole carriage was not so serious as could have been desired, being often mixed with needless laughter.'[378]

This was hardly a friendly letter given all that Whitefield had done for the Wesleys. Whitefield took this latest attack on his character and faith with his usual resignation, but Bennet was not happy that John Wesley was expecting to benefit from the work of Calvinistic Methodist preachers while seeking to muzzle them. He reacted strongly when he heard John was saying once more that he wanted Bennet to continue preaching to his societies but only if he ceased upholding Calvinism. He wrote to Wesley:

'I am not conscious that I preach controversy, or anything but Jesus Christ, simply, practically, and him crucified... If your brethren in point of conscience were in time past constrained to forbid me the [preaching] desk (as at Manchester, etc) because I preached in error heresy, or, as one of them lately said, the devil's doctrine, I am surprised how they can think to profit by me... Wherein you see I'm wrong, I hope you'll use the same freedom I now take, and show me my error.' [379]

John's desire to control the revival was evident also at this time in his very limited dealings with Charles, who was working for the revival but not under John's direction. His unhappiness that Charles was preaching without reference to him surfaced in a letter he sent to his brother on 20 October:

378 28 May 1753 The letter has survived in a copied but endorsed version now in John Rylands Library. See Letters 1740-1755 (edit. F Baker) Vol 26 of Works of JW, Clarendon Press 1982 pg507-8. Charles Wesley did not share John's view on Whitefield's behaviour. Looking back on his contribution Charles later wrote: 'I rejoiced to hear of the great good Mr Whitefield has done in our societies. He preached as universally as my brother... He beat down the separating spirit, highly commended the prayers and services of our Church, charged our people to meet their bands and classes constantly, and never to leave the Methodists or God would leave them.' CWJ 25 Oct 1756.
379 MS Letter Book of John Bennet, John Rylands Library

'Either act in connexion with me, or never pretend to it... I mean take counsel with me once or twice a year as to the places where you will labour.... At present you are so far from this that I do not even know when and where you intend to go; so far are you from following any advice of mine – nay, even from asking it.' [380]

Charles' response was to annotate the letter with the words: 'Trying to bring me under his yoke'.[381] The relationship between the two brothers was only restored when John was taken seriously ill and it was thought he was going to die. In this crisis Charles went to London to sit by his brother's bed and for the first time they spoke properly about what had happened with regard to Grace. On 3 December Charles wrote to Sally to inform her of the good news that he and John had restored their former friendship and agreed to put behind them all that had happened. Although their relationship was never to return to what it had once been, the worst days of the divide between them were over.

---

380 20 Oct 1753 Ms at Emory University transcribed in F. Baker, Letters Vol 26, Works of JW, Clarendon Press 1982 pg526-7

381 ibid

John Wesley as painted by Frank Salisbury (reproduced with the permission of The Trustees of Wesley's Chapel, City Road, London).

Grace Murray as she looked in old age (reproduced with the permission of The Trustees of Wesley's Chapel, City Road, London).

210

10

GRACE'S LATER LIFE

In the summer of 1753 Bennet decided he no longer wished to preach in Bolton in the Methodist building that he had created. On 3 September he leased land on which Whitefield had preached and commenced to build what became known as Duke's Alley Chapel, which was for 'the use of a congregation of Protestant Dissenters'.[382] It was essentially just a large room with small leaded windows, furnished with benches, but, when it opened early in 1754, it attracted not only some of the Methodists loyal to him but also parts of the congregation from the parish church of St Peters and from a nearby Presbyterian Church.[383] The local vicar, Edward Whitehead, decided to try and destroy Bennet's reputation by spreading rumours that he was a bigamist and living in 'uncleaness' with Grace.[384] Bennet strongly refuted the charge and told Whitehead:

'Why should you be so warm? I can assure you that I have no design to hurt you in your trade at Bolton... I have not yet begun to trade upon my own bottom.'[385]

This was said because at this stage Bennet was still travelling widely and sometimes for quite long distances. For example, he had agreed

---

382 W.H. Davison, Centenary Memorials of Duke's Alley Chapel, Bolton 1854 pg 48

383 The latter joined the Chapel because their new minister Thomas Dixon was a Unitarian and opposed to Calvinist thinking, unlike Bennet.

384 Bennet letter to E. Whitehead 18 Feb 1754 Bennet's Letter Book John Rylands Library

385 Bennet letter to E. Whitehead 19 Feb 1754 Bennet's Letter Book John Rylands Library

to preach once a month in Chester at the request of William James, a preacher in the Welsh Calvinistic Association.[386]

Bennet's health had always been poor. His journal reveals how he suffered from terrible headaches, frequent fevers, stomach upsets, kidney stones, and some form of cancer, and the demands of itinerant preaching had further weakened his constitution. A change of pace was vital. On 23 August he consulted the dissenting minister James Clegg, whom he had known since his childhood and who was still the minister at Chinley. Clegg later wrote:

'[I] advised him to desist from preaching from place to place among the Methodists and settle with some society and receive ordination as a Dissenting minister and he told me he would do so.' [387]

Others had also advised Bennet to seek ordination and Whitefield's departure for a fifth preaching tour in America may possibly have been another factor in Bennet's decision to cease itinerant preaching and drop his links with the Methodist movement altogether. He also wanted to spend more time with Grace and his young family.

He therefore applied to the authorities to obtain recognition as a dissenting minister. His Methodist connections led to his request being twice refused, first at the Quarter sessions in Bakewell and then at the Quarter Sessions in Chesterfield. James Clegg then intervened, writing a testimonial in favour of Bennet to the dissenter Sir Henry Hoghton, a justice of the peace and a former M.P. for Preston. Hoghton ensured that Bennet was accepted. The necessary oaths were administered without any opposition at all and a certificate was given. This enabled Bennet, on 9 November, to be

386 Bennet's correspondence indicates he found Chester a very difficult place because of the squabbling between different factions within the city and he did not therefore maintain the monthly visits.

387 Diary of James Clegg 1708-55 Part 3 (edit, V.S.Doe), Derbyshire Record Society 1981 pg 865

officially recognised as the dissenting minister at a small meeting-house that had been opened in the spring at Warburton in Cheshire, six miles east of Warrington. It was a place he had visited for many years and which, although small, had a large and committed congregation, which included Robert Whitton, the man who had collected Jackey Murray from Kingswood.[388] It is interesting that he chose Warburton over a more important centre like Bolton. A factor in that decision may have been that he and Grace would not be subject there to any further controversy. Unlike Edward Whitehead in Bolton, its curate, Timothy Featherstone, was not hostile and regarded Bennet as a friend.

The Bennets were not isolated in their new position. He continued to preach at least four or five times a week further afield. In particular he maintained contact with religious societies in Woodley, Stockport and Millington. It is also thought he preached at nearby Thelwall Hall. A number of families in various places, especially Bolton, brought their children to Warburton to be baptised. This led Bennet to write a book on the subject of infant baptism and he records the names of fifty-four children he baptised between 1754 and 1759. Grace had two more sons, Norman and Joseph, both of whom were baptised in the Independent Chapel in Chinley, which their father had attended as a boy.[389] Unfortunately Bennet badly injured his leg in the summer of 1758 and he lost a lot of blood. Weakened by years of excessive work, he developed jaundice. Grace nursed him for thirty-six weeks but to no avail. She had never entirely abandoned her belief in salvation for all, and so, when it became obvious that he was dying, she asked him whether he still stood by his Calvinist doctrine. He replied ' Yes, ten thousand

388 Bennet visited Warburton at least every two months in the years 1748-9 and monthly 1750-51. In a letter to George Whitefield written around 1750, he referred to the large congregation that existed there and how most of them met regularly in classes and bands.

389 Norman on 23 March 1757 and Joseph on 19 January 1759.

souls; it is the everlasting truth, stick to it.'[390]

Bennet died on 24 May 1759 at the age of just forty-five. Grace wrote:

> 'I have seen... many saints take their leave of this world, but none like JB. May my last end be like his! As I was sitting by his bedside, he said, 'My dear, I am dying'. This was about eleven o'clock and he conversed with me till two. I said, 'Thou art not afraid of dying?' He answered cheerfully, 'No, my dear, for I am assured, past a doubt or even a scruple, that I shall be with the Lord to behold his glory; the blood of Jesus Christ hath cleansed me from all sin. I long to be dissolved. Come, Lord Jesus, loose me from the prison of this clay! O sweet, sweet dying! I could die ten thousand times; too sweet, my dear, too sweet!'[391]

Bennet prayed for her and their children, for his father and sister and her children, and for the Church. Then he said 'I am full – my cup runneth over; sing, sing, yea shout for joy' and Grace says 'We then kissed each other, and he fell asleep in the arms of Jesus with sing, sing, sing.'[392]

Even if Bennet had not been her first choice as a husband, she had always liked and respected him and, as her later writings indicate, she had grown to deeply love him. He was, in the words of her son:

> 'A truly evangelical minister, a faithful witness to the truth, an amiable example of its gracious influence, and one that was eminently owned of God in turning many unto righteousness.'[393]

---

390 GBM pg 23. Many Calvinists believed only 10,000 would be saved.
391 ibid
392 ibid
393 GBM pg 22

His body was buried in the ground of the independent chapel at Chinley. Grace wrote:

'He was lamented both by rich and poor. He was an upright man, and without guile; a lover of all good men. He feared no man, neither would he suffer sin upon his brother. We have sung the praises of God together in our journey below, and we shall sing them together to all eternity.'[394]

Grace thus became a widow again. As far as we can tell, she still had Jackey Murray as well as her four sons by Bennet to look after and so she moved to a house in the main street (now Terrace Road) of Chapel-en-le-Frith in order to be near to her husband's relatives in nearby Chinley. This was not initially an easy move:

'When I came to live at C --- I promised myself great pleasure amongst the people of God. I proposed to several to set up private meetings amongst the women for prayer and religious conference, but they all made excuses. This was a grief to me, yea, it hurt my spirit, and caused me to go into mourning many days. The spirit that was amongst them was quite different to what I had been used to. There was such stiffness and shyness in their looks, as if they would say, 'Stand by, we are holier than you'. If I had not known in whom I believed and something of my own heart, I might have thought their religion all a delusion and been turned out of the way. But, blessed be God, he kept me from taking offence. He knew my aim was right. Therefore I persevered in going amongst them to hear the gospel.' [395]

---

394 GBM pg 23-4
395 She recalled this time in an entry in her journal on 27 Aug 1793

Her later memoirs make no mention of Jackey and so what happened to him is not known. According to her son William, she was a devoted mother to him and his brothers and set them a strong example through the faith that she daily showed:

'[She] not only cheerfully encountered many temporal difficulties in the education of her children... but also, by her example, her counsels, her prayers, her pleasing converse, and her prudent care, trained them up in the nurture and admonition of the Lord. Reading the word of God, singing his praises, and calling on his name with her family, morning and evening, were daily practised in her house; and these things were always done with such reverence, spirituality, and fervour, as could not help convincing every one that witnessed them, how deeply her heart was engaged in them. She was never tedious in the length of religious services, to render them a burden; and through all she introduced that agreeable variety, which made them entertaining, as well as impressive. Few Christians possessed so eminently the spirit and gift of prayer. In her chamber she daily spent a considerable time in secret converse with God: the throne of grace was truly her asylum, whither she fled in all circumstances of trouble and perplexity.'[396]

She rose early so she could have time to study herself and, rather than engaging in lots of social gossip, read widely, not just devotional works but also history books and poetry. She thought social chit chat too often 'murders time and leaves the mind empty and dissipated'.[397]

Grace faced further personal tragedy because she lost three of her sons by Bennet. It is not known exactly what happened to

396 GBM pg 24-5 This reads almost like a description of Susanna Wesley and it is not surprising that John Wesley would have been drawn to want a wife who was so like his own mother.
397 GBM pg 25

Norman but the two-year old Joseph died in November 1761 and the twelve-year old John in December 1762. She became a regular visitor to those who were sick and her son William later wrote:

'The inhabitants in general looked up to her, on such occasions, with peculiar veneration and confidence, as a mother in Israel, who knew how to speak a word in season; and even such as in health were carnal and profane, would hearken to her advice, and request her prayers, in their time of illness, with great humility and earnestness. She was always ready to fall in with such calls of Providence; and several instances are within my own recollection of persons, who, by her instrumentality, were truly awakened, and brought to the knowledge of the truth, and died full of peace and good hope towards God.'[398]

She joined the Methodist society, worshipping at the Town End Chapel and holding meetings in her house. Her son wrote:

'My father having been accustomed frequently to preach in his own house to such of the neighbours as attended, after his death she endeavoured to provide for the continuance of their instruction by inviting Gospel ministers at a distance, to come and preach in rotation at her house, where they always received a kind and respectful entertainment. She had also weekly meetings for prayer and religious conversation, both of a general and a more select nature, which in great measure she herself conducted, and which proved a great blessing to the souls of many.'[399]

398 GBM pg 26
399 ibid

That Grace had lost none of her evangelistic fervour is illustrated by the following story that was told about her, although its veracity cannot be proved. In March 1764 it is said Grace heard that John Wesley was going to be preaching in the Mulberry Street Chapel in Sheffield and she decided to go and hear him, even though this meant travelling on her own. En route she overtook a churchwarden and they happily agreed to continue the journey together. They engaged in conversation and the subject of Methodism came up. When the churchwarden began to swear offensively against it, Grace reproved him. When he threatened to horsewhip her she defiantly said he would have to obtain God's permission first. He sarcastically asked what she knew about God. In reply Grace stated her trust in God and invited him to attend the Methodist meeting with her. To her surprise he did and she was pleased to see that the experience reduced him to tears.

With very little income it must have been a harsh life but Grace never tried to remarry because she felt nobody could take Bennet's place. Her father-in-law, William Bennet, died in October 1766 at the age of eighty-eight but she still had the support of Robert Bennet, a relative of her husband who lived in Chinley, and she doubtless took pleasure in his growing family.[400] It was a cause of sadness when Robert died in 1780. Grace admitted to a minister in 1785 how much she missed her husband:

'Without the enjoyment of his love everything is poor and empty... I had a husband one in a thousand, an upright man he spent his life in the Lord's cause'.[401]

She also said that she also still loved and honoured John Wesley 'as a

---

400 He had six children: John (Aug 1764), William (Aug 1766), Robert (July 1769), Sarah (Dec 1771), Joseph (July 1774) and James (Aug 1777). His wife died following the birth of the last child.
401 Letter to Rev. Manning of Hoxton 3 Sept 1785 MAM PLP 8.81.1 John Rylands Library

father' and that she doubted not but he, she and her husband would 'spend a happy eternity together'.[402]

One of her remaining joys was the career of her remaining son from her marriage with Bennet. William became a co-pastor at a dissenting chapel in London at Moorfields in 1778. This was known as the Meeting House on the Pavement. As a boy William had gone to the local grammar school in Chapel-en-le-Frith and then boarded at a farm in Astley in Lancashire so he could attend a school run by a distant relative of the Bennet family. He had then been taught by a dissenting minister called Plumbe, who lived in Charlesworth in Derbyshire, before going to the Independent College, Homerton, a small dissenting academy just outside London, in 1772.[403] The college's distinguished theological tutor and president was Dr John Condor, the pastor at the chapel in Moorfields. William proved highly successful in Moorfields and took over as pastor when Condor died in 1781.[404] He was described as having 'a mind cultivated by education' and an imagination that was 'brilliant and lively in the highest degree'.[405] In 1784 he married Esther Shrimpton, who came from a Quaker family in High Wycombe, and they had two children. Sadly both died and so did Esther in February 1787.

This may have been why Grace went to stay with William for a time in his house in Colebrook Row. She was there in 1788, the year of Charles Wesley's death, and probably attended her son's second marriage to Mary Ewer in September. At some time during her stay she sent a note to John Wesley via the lay preacher Thomas Olivers,

402 ibid

403 It was one of the thirty-five academies set up after the government had banned dissenters from studying at Oxford and Cambridge. It only catered for between twelve and twenty students but it had a high reputation. It was later to evolve into Homerton College, Cambridge.

404 When William Bennet died an obituary appeared in the Congregational Magazine and it said of him that as a preacher 'he attained an unusual degree of popularity in the metropolis' and that he was also noted for his 'diligent attention to pastoral duties'. London Christian Instructor No 61 Jan 1823 pg 5

405 ibid pg 2

possibly to commiserate him on the loss of his brother. At that time Olivers was working with John on editing material for Methodist publications, notably the Arminian Magazine, but he had known Grace back in the 1740s.[406] Her letter asked if John would come and see her. He agreed to go to her son William's house and one of those present, Henry Moore, later commented on how her sweetness of spirit was such that it made him realise why John Wesley had loved her so much. He says John 'preserved more than his usual self-possession' throughout their meeting and never mentioned her after it, but repeatedly said the hand of God had been at work in ensuring his unhappy marriage to Molly Vazeille. Her less loving nature had ensured that he was never distracted from giving all his attention to the work of the revival:

> 'He believed the Lord over-ruled this whole painful business for his good; and that, if Mrs Wesley had been a better wife, he might have been unfaithful to the great work to which God had called him, and might have too much sought to please her according to her own views.'[407]

It was a view that others had expressed over the years. John Berridge, Vicar of Everton, for example, in 1770 wrote to the Countess of Huntingdon:

> '[There is] no trap so mischievous to the field preacher as wedlock... Matrimony has quite maimed poor Charles [Wesley], and might have spoiled John [Wesley] and George [Whitefield], if a wise master had not graciously sent them a pair of ferrets [as

---

406 Wesley regarded Olivers as a close friend and used him as an editor even though he was not sufficiently well-educated to always be effective in that role. Today Olivers is best-remembered for his hymn, 'The God of Abraham praise'.

407 H. Moore, Life of JW, London 1825 Vol II pg 175

their wives]'. [408]

It also ties in with a letter that John Wesley wrote in 1789 to a preacher who had escaped matrimony at the last minute. He informed the preacher that God had prevented him marrying the woman he loved and that was to prevent him from being distracted:

> 'You send me good news indeed. I congratulate you upon your deliverance. It is not a little one. Only He that is almighty was able to burst those bonds asunder. Many years ago I was exactly in the same case and... [when I read in the Bible] 'Son of Man, behold I take from thee the desire of thine eyes with a stroke' I was quite stunned... But afterwards I saw God was wiser than me... Remember the wise direction of [Thomas a] Kempis, 'Avoid all good women, and commend them to God.'[409]

Grace's new daughter-in-law came from quite a wealthy family. Her father was an orange merchant of Lincoln's Inn Fields and she had inherited a fortune of £10,000. This proved fortunate when William Bennet was forced to retire in February 1793, after a year of serious ill health. William chose to return to Derbyshire, probably so he could look after his mother. He purchased Stoddard Lodge, near Chapel-en-le-Frith. This was the former home of James Clegg, who had been the Bennet family's minister for many years. William undertook some local preaching but it was always at 'the hazard of his health' because his illness appears to have left him with a problem with the muscles in his chest.[410] Grace loved being so near to her son and daughter-in-law:

---

408 23 March 1770 transcribed in The British Critic and Quartely Theological Review London 1840 Vol XXVIII pg 291
409 J. Telford, Letters of JW, Epworth 1931 Vol VIII pg 116
410 London Christian Instructor or Congregational Magazine No 62 Feb 1823 pg 60. Bennet died in 1821.

'The Lord had had pity on me and sent my dear W[illiam] and his other self, who is as tender over me as my own daughter, to be a comfort in my old age. I can truly say I have had more comfort these six months than I had for thirty-four years.'[411]

She continued to hold band and class meetings in her home as well as prayer meetings. Her life was still marked by frequent mood swings. Sometimes she felt depressed and overwhelmed with gloom. At other times she was full of joy and hope. Always she preached about the importance of not believing you could earn your salvation because that came as a gift from God. In the diary that she kept between 1792 and 1800 her faith shines through on almost every page. Here, for example, is her prayer for the start of a new year:

'Help me, Lord, to begin this new year with thee! O my God, fulfil all thy pleasure in and by me, the most unworthy of all thy servants! Yet I would love thee, thou knowest: I can appeal unto thee, I would rather die, than sin against thee.'[412]

And here a reflective passage on those who have fallen away from their faith:

'O Lord, quicken me to run the way of thy commandments! How doth my soul mourn for some that did begin well, but now seem to be swallowed up of the world! I hope I have delivered my own soul, yet I will weep for them in secret places. I pray God embitter every sinful sweet, and hedge up their way with thorns, rather than they should run into destruction! It is not beginning well, but finishing!'[413]

411 29 Oct 1793 GBM pg 47
412 1 Jan 1792 GBM pg 29
413 4 March 1792 GBM pg 32

Prayer remained very important to her:

'How sweet is it to enjoy communion with God! One drop of the love of God makes full amends for all our trials. I would rather have a sense of this… than enjoy all the riches of both the Indies, yea, than all worlds… Is it not true of every Christian when he has been conversing with God (if the intercourse has been open between God and the soul) that he afterwards shines in humility, meekness, love, and spiritual mindedness?'[414]

So too did helping people:

'We were not sent into the world for our own sakes alone, but for the good of others, as far as we have ability. We should therefore consider what place we are in, whether an eye, or a hand, or a foot in the body of Christ, and act as such.'[415]

Having suffered at their hands over the years, she had no time for those who preferred gossiping:

'Backbiters and talebearers are Satan's agents… Such I would not have enter my house… Indeed, this is a sin we should flee from, as from the face of a serpent. I can truly say I have been pained to my heart by hearing evilspeaking… I have been blamed for speaking too little in company, but I would rather err on that hand, than by speaking too much… If we had a sense of the divine presence, we should be more cautious both of what we speak and do.' [416]

414 19 Feb and 30 Nov 1792 GBM pg 31 and 39
415 27 May 1792 GBM pg 36
416 1 Sept 1793 GBM pg 42-3

On her own situation she wrote:

'I cannot say that I find those transports of joy, which I have experienced in times past; but, I bless God, I find a solid hope, that enables me to rest my all upon the atonement made by the Lamb: there will I trust my soul; yea, ten thousand souls if I had them.'[417]

Despite her years with Bennet, Grace often writes things that do not appear to have the kind of certainty normally associated with Calvinism. For example, she is often highly critical of her shortcomings and her mood swings, and sometimes of her lack of faith:

'Unbelief is the torment of my soul... O that I could simply believe what the Lord has said to me!.... How long shall I grieve God by making him as changeable as myself! Wretch that I am, it is a wonder God does not cut me off, and cast me into hell!.... The Lord doth often comfort my soul with the consolations of his Spirit. But still I am afraid when these comforts are gone, lest they are not from the Spirit of God.'[418]

All she wanted was to make sure that at the end 'I may have my loins girt, my lamp trimmed, and my light shining!' [419] Despite her self-criticism, it is obvious that Grace had an assurance that God was going to forgive her and offer her eternal happiness when her life ended. After the death of a friend, she wrote:

'I took my leave of her the night before she died, believing we

417 24 June 1793 GBM pg 41
418 6 Dec 1796 GBM pg 66
419 25 Dec 1792 GBM pg 40

should meet again at the right hand of God: how soon, God knoweth. O Lord, make me ready! Then, no matter how soon. May I live every day as my last! .... What is death, but the door into eternity? My dear Saviour has entered, and taken possession for me, and has told me, that where he is, there I shall be also, to behold his glory. Hallelujah!'[420]

Perhaps the most moving image she gives of her readiness to step into eternity comes in a passage written after she had recovered from an illness that she thought was going to kill her:

'I was countermanded when I thought myself in sight of my port, with my sails spread, and filled with the gales of the Divine Spirit. How have I seen, when I have been upon the ocean, a ship with all her sails unfurled, and right before the wind, the mariners rejoicing, and myself with them, thinking we were so near our desired haven; when suddenly a cross wind has sprung up, and blown us quite away to another port, and that for several days! So am I.'[421]

In some of the extended passages one gets a glimpse into what she must have been like when she preached:

'Some, I fear, are content to get so much religion as will save them from the fear of hell; but in this, they are woefully deceiving themselves; for true religion not only saves from the fear of hell, but it makes truly happy, and works a crucifixion in us to this vain world, with all its delusive joys. Where God has taken possession of the heart, he takes away the love of all those

---

420 14 May 1792 GBM pg 35-6
421 25 Dec 1792 GBM pg 40

things that once led us captive… All the love that such persons regarded other things with before, is turned to the love of God; and it is their grief that they cannot love him more and serve him better: I am sure it is mine; and I believe true grace has the same effect in all.'[422]

There are many incidences in her writing of pithy comments: 'Words are not prayer'[423]; 'I would love much, having had much forgiven'[424]; 'Be swift to hear and slow to speak' [425]; '[A Christian] should be at all times cheerful, without levity, solid, without surliness'[426]; 'I hate excuses both in myself and others'[427]; 'If there can be mourning in heaven, I shall lament my unfaithfulness and short-comings to eternity'[428]; 'We should act faith when we think we have no faith' [429]; and 'I have poured out all my [com]plaints and tears and I believe God has put them in his bottle.'[430]

The later entries in her diary are often reflections on her growing frailty and on her life as a widow and how she wished she could be in heaven with Bennet and able to see God 'without a veil'.[431] At times when she was not feeling well she consoled herself with what she had done when younger: 'I have had glorious seasons in my Lord's vineyards'.[432] There are two clear references to her feelings about Wesley. After his death she re-read his journal and wrote:

422 8 Oct 1793 GBM pg 45-6
423 1 Feb 1792 GBM pg 31
424 14 April 1792 GBM pg 34
425 1 Sept 1793 GBM pg 43
426 4 Oct 1793 GBM pg 45
427 20 Jan 1796 GBM pg 61
428 ibid
429 22 March 1796 GBM pg 63
430 19 Aug 1799 GBM pg 78
431 24 May 1794 GBM pg 54
432 9 Nov 1794 GBM pg 57

'How did I lament in calling to mind those happy days in the church he mentions! For I was an eye and ear-witness of those persons God was pleased to work upon in that extraordinary way.[433]

After reading the first biography of Wesley, she commented that she never looked back with regret on the time that she had spent with him:

'I bless God I was ever under his discipline. I knowed his manner of life and conversation as well as most having... travelled by sea and land.... I shall meet him again as he told me in his last letter; 'we have spent many happy days together'. I doubt it not.' [434]

The timing of his last letter is not given and Grace may be referring back to a letter written many years before, but it is possible that they had entered into some correspondence that has not survived.

By the summer of 1795 she was saying 'my clay cottage begins to totter', but, although she was ready to die, she was content to wait on God's timing.[435] Like all old people, she had good days and bad days and she reflected philosophically on the mood changes that had dogged her all her life:

'The Christian's life is justly called a warfare, uphill and down; I find my frames often changing; one hour I am full of peace and comfort, the next I am stripped and emptied, as if I knew nothing of heavenly things: I cannot assign the reason for this, but I believe it is the way God is pleased ... to make us sensible

---

433 19 Oct 1793 GBM pg 46
434 17 March 1798. This was written after she had read a biography of Wesley
435 5 September 1795 GBM pg 58

that all our help is from him.'[436]

By 1798 she was saying 'my cottage of clay [is] coming down fast'[437] and she wrote in June:

'I have been in the school of Christ nearly sixty years; and the nearer I approach eternity, the more I see my need of a complete Saviour. Oh, how I admire the glorious plan of redemption by the Son of God ! O Lord Jesus, I would lie in the dust before thee: may my desires to love thee be accepted ! Amen.'[438]

And in September of that year:

'I bless God, I feel a revival in my dry, drooping soul. I have had a long winter season, and all through reasoning. If Satan can bring us to pore upon our own hearts, till we lose the sight and sense of Christ's fullness, he gains his end. This, the Lord knows, I am now saying from bitter experience. Yes, in deep waters hath my soul travailed; through floods of temptations have I passed; but out of them all the Lord has brought me. He hath again set my feet upon himself, the Rock of ages; and I doubt not. How tenderly doth my heavenly Father deal with me, so unworthy. I feel my bodily strength and all my faculties decline more within these three months, than for a twelvemonth before. I can rejoice that my journey is almost over. Methinks I sometimes see those that once were my companions here, but now inheriting mansions above, stand waiting their Lord's command to go and fetch their sister-spirit home. I doubt not of

---

436 28 Nov 1795 GBM pg 61
437 17 March 1798 GBM pg 73
438 28 June 1798 GBM pg 73

our joyful meeting.'[439]

As her health further declined, she increasingly looked back with fondness on the time when she had been young and fit:

'My happiest days where when I rose at 4 o'clock for prayer, and preaching at five. I find it no cross at this day (being in my 84th year) to rise early to wait upon God with his people, no more than when I was thirty.'[440]

Yet she still retained an interest in what was going on in the world, commenting, for example, in her diary on Nelson's victory over the French fleet in the Battle of the Nile. She continued to run her class meeting until at least 1799 because she wrote in August of that year:

'Class meeting at my house. It was a good time – the Lord was present. We seemed all one heart. It is a pleasant thing and desirable for brethren of any community to be joined in heart and mind that we may strive together for the hope of the gospel. They all agreed to meet at my house once a fortnight out of pity to me being so confined.'[441]

At the turn of a new century she wrote:

'I have lived to enter upon another century, and am now nearly eighty-five years of age – a wonder to myself and to many! But why should we wonder? Is it not God that gave me life? And has he not a right to continue it so long as it will be for his glory? For

439 19 Sept 1798 GBM pg 74-5
440 13 May 1799 GBM pg 78
441 19 Aug 1799 Item 328 Bennet Box John Rylands Library

what cause I am spared is best known to my heavenly Father.' [442]

She ceased writing the diary on 23 June 1800. Her sight had become too impaired and her hands too crippled to easily hold a pen. She could no longer see well enough to read her Bible, although this had been her greatest daily pleasure. Her family and friends offered to read to her, but she told them she thanked God that he had inspired her to read the scriptures so much that the entire book was stored in her memory and so she could still engage in daily reflection unassisted. She continued to offer advice and help to others:

'Young persons of both sexes flocked around her for spiritual advice, showing the sincerest affection and reverence for her as a mother in Israel; and for these she entertained a reciprocal love and esteem, having no greater joy, than to see them walking in the truth. As she had a very deep experience in the things of God, and an extensive acquaintance among his people, she was eminently fitted to be an instructor of babes, and a comforter of them that mourn. This was her delightful work, even to the last. She made it the serious business of her days.'[443]

At the start of 1803 it became obvious that Grace had not much longer to live. On 22 February, after a very painful and restless night, she told those who were caring for her:

'Blessed be God, I have peace... I have had wonderful manifestations of God to my soul, far beyond many. But I have always been afraid of saying too much, rather than too little, wishing rather that my life and conversation should witness

442 17 Jan 1800 GBM pg 78-9
443 GBM pg 81

to the truth of my profession… I am a sinner, saved freely by grace… Some people I have heard speak much of our being faithful to the grace of God, as if they rested much on their own faithfulness. I never could bear this. It is God's faithfulness to his own word of promise that is my security for salvation.'[444]

During the course of that night she deteriorated greatly but remained strong in her faith:

'By the motions of her lips and eyes, as well as by the words she uttered occasionally, it appeared that she was continually conversing with God, and commending her departing spirit into His hands who had redeemed her. Several times she repeated with great sensibility these words: 'When will his chariot wheels advance, to call his exiled home? Sweet Jesus, come quickly, and set my soul at rest!' ' [445]

It has been said that the only lasting absorbing passion of John Wesley was his love of God but maybe that could also be said of Grace Bennet. To his edition of her memoirs her son William appended a hymn that she had written years before and which he had found among his father's papers. It is undated but it reflects the readiness she had shown throughout her life to always put God first:

'Lift up your eyes to Sion's hill,
ye followers of the Lamb;
who in one mind and spirit strive
and for the faith contend.
'Courage!', your Captain cries, 'be strong,

nor fear to win the day;
tho' death and hell should both combine
to take your crown away.

My promise stands for ever sure,
and never shall remove;
Believe, look up, and hear my voice,
Be steadfast in my love.

You shall o'ercome, through strength divine,
and more than conquerors be;
in patience then possess your souls,
and always look to me.'

O let us all with one consent,
My fellow soldiers dear,
In patient hope keep looking up,
till Christ our head appear.

And let us lawfully contend,
and for the prize pursue;
and take the crown that Christ has won,
and wear it as our due.' [446]

On 23 February Grace briefly seemed to rally and she told her son 'Glory be to God, Jesus is mine and I am his, and that's enough for me!'[447]. She then weakened again and died at midnight. Her last words were: 'Glory be to thee, my God: peace thou givest me!' [448] She was eighty-eight.

446 GBM pg 86-7
447 GBM pg 85
448 ibid

Grace's funeral service was taken by Dr Jabez Bunting, one of the most prominent of the ministers in the newly created Methodist Church that had emerged following the death of John Wesley. He used the text from Psalm 27 that she had requested: 'I should utterly have fainted but that I believe verily to see the goodness of the Lord in the land of the living'. She was buried alongside the remains of her beloved husband at Chinley Chapel and the register of her death contains perhaps her best epitaph:

'She was a real pious saint of Christ for 63 years'.

Print showing the plaque that commemorates John and Charles Wesley in Westminster Abbey (New Room)

Epilogue:
A NOTE ON SOURCES

The main source of information on Grace Murray is contained in a manuscript that gives John Wesley's version of events. It is in the handwriting of an amanuensis, but there are several corrections in John's handwriting. It is probably a copy of what John wrote in November 1749 for his sister-in-law, Sally Wesley, and therefore written very much in the heat of the moment. Clearly it is therefore biased. It was intended to portray how God had specially prepared Grace to become his wife and how fair-minded and forbearing he had been towards her and John Bennet, only to have his own brother prevent his marriage for spurious reasons. Charles understandably objected to his wife being given it to read. Even if one does not accept all that John Wesley says at face value, the manuscript undoubtedly provides us with a deep insight into what happened. It is by far the most deeply personal account of his feelings that he ever produced and, unlike most of his writing, it does not bear the signs of having been carefully edited for publication. It also gives us a detailed account of Grace's early life because it includes what Wesley describes as a verbatim transcription by him of what Grace Murray had told him whilst the two of them were staying together in Berwick-on-Tweed in September 1748.

The manuscript was donated to the British Museum in 1829 in the will of Napthaly Hart, whose home was in Islington. Attached to the manuscript was a lengthy poem that John had written whilst travelling between Leeds and Newcastle immediately after Grace's marriage. It is in his handwriting and its authenticity has never been questioned. Hart claimed that he had obtained both documents from Noah Vazeille, the step-son of John Wesley after Vazeille had revealed its existence to him in 1788. It is not clear how the manuscript came into Noah's hands but presumably he acquired it from his mother's papers after her death. It has been suggested that Wesley may have given the manuscript to Molly just as he gave a copy to Sally Wesley, although it is difficult to see why he would think reading such a document would improve his relationship with his wife! It is perhaps more likely that Molly Vazeille simply stole it. She used to search though her husband's possessions and take some of his correspondence. Why did she keep it? Presumably because it was proof of her allegation that John had never loved her when he had married her. Indeed, the document may well have played a part in the break up of their marriage.

In 1848 the manuscript was transcribed by Charles Hook, a professional copier of manuscripts, and published as a 'Narrative of a remarkable transaction in the early life of John Wesley from an original manuscript in his own handwriting, never before published.' There were only five hundred copies produced and eventually a second edition was published in 1862. However, Hook's transcription altered and cut the original and it was not until 1910 that the scholar Augustin Leger made a fully accurate and complete rendition. Dent published this under the title 'Wesley's Lost Love'. This book also contained a lengthy account of Wesley's marriage to Molly Vazeille written by Leger. My footnotes refer to Leger's transcription as JWLL. I used the copy of his book that is in the John Rylands Library, but a copy in Cornell University Library has recently been made available in an online edition and this has given potential readers easier access.

We know that both Charles Wesley and John Bennet wrote accounts of what happened from their perspective but these have not survived. John Wesley's account has therefore to be looked at alongside the other evidence that we have – this includes the published journals of John and Charles Wesley and the fragments that have survived of John Bennet's diary. The problem with the published version of John Wesley's journal is that he included only what he wanted people to know and it is therefore highly selective in what it chooses to say. There are many editions of John Wesley's Journal and so, when I have quoted from it, I have stated JWJ and simply given the relevant date of entry in the footnotes rather than specifying a particular edition and pagination.

In Charles Wesley's case, he kept his daily record just on loose bits of paper and he subsequently began editing these into a version from which he could then produce a publishable version if at some stage that was deemed useful. The original papers have been lost and, when his uncompleted material was transcribed in the nineteenth century, not even all of the edited version could be included because Charles had written certain passages in a secret code. When I originally started studying Grace Murray I used the edition of Charles' journal produced by Thomas Jackson in 1849. I have stated CWJ when quoting this. However, S.T. Kimbrough and K.G.C. Newport produced a new edition of his journal in two volumes in 2008 and it was published by Kingswood Press under the title 'The Manuscript Journal of the Reverend Charles Wesley. Most of it confirms the accuracy of Jackson's earlier work but there are some very significant changes, the most notable being that its editors decoded the secret passages. I have indicated next to CWJ if the particular extract is part of the coded manuscript which can only be found in the new edition, which is undoubtedly the definitive version of his journal. I thoroughly recommend anyone with an interest in Charles Wesley reading both volumes.

John Bennet's diary has many gaps and what exists is held in the collections of the John Rylands Library and Drew University Library. These were fully transcribed by S.R. Valentine and published by the now defunct Methodist Publishing House in 2002 under the title 'Mirror of the Soul: the Diary of an early Methodist Preacher'. It is referenced as JBD in the footnotes. Valentine prior to that produced the first major biography of the preacher entitled 'John Bennet and the Origins of Methodism and the Evangelical Revival' (published in 1997 by the Scarecrow Press) and it is still the only definitive biography of him. Very few historians have devoted time to serious study of a Wesleyan lay preacher and this is a notable exception – and well worth reading.

An edited version of Grace's memoirs, together with extracts from her diaries, was produced by her son William after her death and published in Macclesfield in 1803 by the printer E. Bayley. It verifies the accuracy of much of Wesley's version of Grace's early life, but the memoirs are doubly censored because not only did William choose what to include and exclude but so too did Grace. The letter to her son in which she left him her papers is printed as a kind of preface to the book and in it she wrote:

> 'I have left some broken hints of my life for you to do with as you shall see good. They are written with great simplicity, but contain the truth. I might have said much more, for I have omitted many things which I passed through… I would rather say less than more, having always been afraid of saying or doing wrong.'

There is nothing within the book on the period when John Wesley was courting Grace and the extracts that are included often stress her later love for John Bennet. Its main value is the information it provides about Grace's life after Bennet died. I have referred to this book as GBM in the footnotes. A copy of the book is in the John Rylands Library but an online edition has been created recently by Emory University.

I have used many other contemporary sources, especially letters, as well as a number of secondary studies and details of all of those are in the footnotes. I am grateful for the assistance I was given by the staff at the John Rylands Library when I first began researching this topic and for their permission to quote from the documents in this book. Since then the letters of Charles Wesley in that library and others held elsewhere in other collections written between 1728 and 1756 have been transcribed and edited by K.G.C. Newport and G. Lloyd and published in The Letters of Charles Wesley Vol I by OUP in 2013. For any student of the period this makes fascinating reading and it is a worthy companion to the volumes of John Wesley's letters contained in the Oxford Edition of the Works of John Wesley produced in the 1980s.

For the sake of completeness, I provide below the entire text of the poem that John Wesley wrote as he travelled from Leeds to Newcastle, having just heard of Grace's marriage to John Bennet:

1. O Lord I bow my sinful head!
 Righteous are all thy ways with man!
 Yet suffer me with thee to plead,
 With lowly reverence to complain,
 With deep, unutter'd grief to groan,
 O what is this that Thou hast done!

2. Oft as thro' giddy youth I rov'd,
 And danced along the flowery way,
 By chance or thoughtless passion mov'd,
 An easy, unsuspicious prey
 I fell, while Love's envenomed dart
 Thrilled thro' my veins, and tore my heart.

3. At length, by sad experience taught,
 Firm I shook off the abject yoke;

Abhor'd his sweetly-poisonous draught,
Thro' all his wily fetters broke;
Fixt my desires on things above,
And languisht for Celestial Love.

4.   Born on the wings of sacred hope
Long had I soar'd, and spurn'd the ground;
When panting for the mountain-top
My soul a kindred spirit found;
By heaven intrusted to my care,
The daughter of my faith and prayer.

5.   In early dawn of life, serene,
Mild, sweet and tender was her mood:
Her pleasing form spoke all within
Soft and compassionately good:
List'ning to every wretch's care,
Mixing with each her friendly tear.

6.   In dawn of life, to feed the poor
Glad she her little all bestow'd:
Wise to lay up a better Store,
And hasting to be rich in God;
God whom she sought with early care,
With reverence and with lowly fear.

7.   E'er twice four years past o'er her head,
Her infant breast with love He fill'd,
His glorious, gracious Name reveal'd,
And sweetly forc'd her heart to yield,
She groan'd to ascend Heaven's high abode,
To die into the arms of God!

8.   Yet warm with youth and beauty's pride,
       Soon was her heedless soul betray'd;
       From Heaven her footsteps turn'd aside,
       O'er pleasure's flowry plains she stray'd:
       Fondly the toys of earth she sought.
       And God was not in all her thought.

9.   Not long. A messenger she saw
       Sent forth glad tidings to proclaim:
       She heard, with joy and wond'ring awe
       His cry: 'Sinners, behold the Lamb!'
       His eye her inmost nature shook.
       His word her heart in pieces broke.

10.   Her bosom heav'd with labouring sighs,
       And groan'd the unutterable prayer;
       As rivers from her streaming eyes
       Fast flow'd the never-ceasing tear,
       Till Jesus spake, 'Thy mourning is o'er!
       Believe! Rejoice! And weep no more.'

11.   She heard: pure love her soul o'erflow'd
       Sorrow and sighing fled away:
       With sacred zeal her spirit glow'd:
       Panting His every word to obey,
       Her faith by plenteous fruit she shew'd,
       And all her works were wrought in God.

12.   Nor works alone her faith approv'd:
       Soon in affliction's furnace tried
       By him whom next to Heaven she lov'd,
       As silver seven times purified,

Shone midst the flames her constant mind,
Emerg'd, and left the dross behind.

13.   When death, in freshest strength of years
Her much-lov'd friend tore from her breast
A while she pour'd her plaints and tears;
But quickly turning to her rest
'Thy will be done!' she meekly cried:
'Suffice, for me the Saviour died.'

14.   When first I view'd with fixt regard
Her artless tears in silence flow,
For thee are better things prepar'd,
I said: 'Go forth, with Jesus go!
My Master's peace be on thy soul,
Till perfect love shall make thee whole.'

15.   But O! what trials are in store
For those whom GOD delights to bless:
Abandon'd soon to Satan's power
Sifted as wheat, from the abyss
The lowest deep she groan'd aloud;
Where is my joy, my hope, my GOD?

16.   In chains of horrid darkness bound,
Torn by the dogs of Hell she lay;
By fear and sin encompast round.
Anguish and pain and huge dismay,
Till the loud, bitter cry outbroke,
'My God, why hast thou me forsook?'

17.   Yet bowing down her fainting head,
     And sinking to the gulf beneath,
     She flew to every sinner's aid,
     To snatch him from the second death:
     'Tho' justly I am lost,' she cried,
     'Live thou! For thee the Saviour died.'

18.   But, when again his glory shone,
     When God anew unveil'd his face,
     What heavenly zeal, what love unknown,
     What strong, unutter'd tenderness,
     For every soul her heart o'erflow'd!
     What longing to be spent for GOD!

19.   I saw her run, with winged speed
     In works of faith and labouring love:
     I saw her glorious toil succeed,
     And showers of blessings from above
     Crowning her warm effectual prayer,
     And glorified my God in her.

20.   Yet while to all, her tender mind
     In streams of pure affection flow'd,
     To one, by ties peculiar join'd,
     One only less belov'd than God,
     'Myself,' she said, 'my soul I owe,
     My guardian angel here below!'

21.   From Heaven the grateful ardour came,
     Pure from the dross of low desire:
     Well-pleas'd I mark'd the guiltless flame,
     Nor dar'd to damp the sacred fire;

Heaven's choicest gift on man bestow'd,
Strength'ning our hearts and hands in GOD.

22.   Twas now I bow'd my aching head,
While sickness shook the house of clay:
Duteous she ran with humble speed,
Love's tenderest offices to pay;
To ease my pain, to soothe my care,
To uphold my feeble hands in pray'r.

23.   Amaz;d I cried, 'Surely for me
An help prepar'd of Heaven thou art!
Thankful I take the gift from Thee,
O Lord, nor ought on earth shall part
The souls whom thou hast join'd above
In lasting bonds of sacred love.'

24.   Abash'd she spake, 'O what is this,
Far above all my boldest hope!
Can God, beyond my utmost wish,
Thus lift his worthless handmaid up?
This only could my soul desire:
This only (had I dar'd) require.'

25.   From that glad hour, with growing love,
Heaven's latest, dearest gift I view'd:
While, pleas'd each moment to improve,
We urg'd our way with strength renew'd.
Our one desire, our common aim,
To extol our gracious Master's name.

26.   Companions now in weal and woe,
       No Power on Earth could us divide:
       Nor summer's heat, nor wintry snow
       Could tear my partner from my side;
       Nor toil, nor weariness, nor pain,
       Nor horrors of the angry main.

27.   Oft, (tho' as yet the nuptial tie
       was not), clasping her hand in mine,
       'What force', she said, 'beneath the sky,
       Can now our well-knit souls disjoin?
       With thee I'd go to India's coast,
       To worlds in distant ocean lost!'

28.   Such was the friend than life more dear
       Whom in one luckless baleful hour,
       (For ever mention'd with a tear)
       The tempest's unresisted power,
       (O the unutterable smart!)
       Tore from my inly-bleeding heart.

29.   Unsearchable thy judgments are,
       O Lord, a bottomless abyss!
       Yet sure thy love, thy guardian care,
       O'er all thy works extended is.
       O why didst thou the blessing send?
       Or why thus snatch away my friend?

30.   What thou hast done I know not now!
       Suffice I shall hereafter know!
       Beneath thy chastning hand I bow:
       That still I live to Thee I owe.

O teach thy deeply-humbled son
To say, 'Father, thy will be done!'

31.   Teach me, from every pleasing snare
To keep the issues of my heart
Be thou my love, my joy, my fear!
Thou my eternal portion art.
Be thou my never-failing friend,
And love, O love me to the End!

This poem still conveys better than any historian just how much John Wesley grieved for his lost love, Grace Murray.